MIRROR, MIRROR

First published in 2016 by Reed Independent, Victoria, Australia.

Printed by Createspace.com, a division of Amazon.com.

Available as a printed book or an ebook from Createspace.com or Amazon.com or Kindle estores, together with most major international online outlets or bookshops with online ordering facilities:
paperback: ISBN 9780994531186
ebook: ISBN 9780994531193

Front cover: Image from Google Images. Design by Dilani Priyangika Ranaweera, Dart Lanka Productions

National Library of Australia Cataloguing-in-Publication entry:
Creator: Reed, Bill, author.
Title: Mirror, Mirror/ Bill Reed
Edition: first
ISBN: 9780994531186 (paperback)
ISBN: 9780994531193 (ebook)
Notes: includes bibliographical reference.
Subjects: Drama/black comedy
Dewey Number: A822.3

MIRROR, MIRROR

a play

Bill Reed

𝓡

First Showings

Concerning the first substance of this play – on which this play included here is loosely based -- the 1978 press release for the Playbox Theatre (now Malthouse Theatre) Season Two read in part:

'A poignant black comedy, 'Talking to a Mirror', is by noted Australian playwright Bill Reed, whose many credits include Bullsh, which was produced by Playbox in 1978. Directed by young Melbourne director Russell Walsh and designed by Michael Scott-Mitchell, 'Talking to a Mirror' opens on November 27 and runs through to October 15'.

Due to assessment and selection by the Australian Script Centre, this script is available on the Centre's website Australianplays.org.

The Characters

This is a play for a recommended five (only) actors.

Because the play employs smoke-and-mirrors for depicting RINNER's delusions, the other actors will double up parts with, hopefully, gay abandon. Their interchanging and timings need not be exact; indeed, they should 'ham' them up as appropriate.

RINNER
He exacts from life exactly as he is... a man stuck between the two cultures of Far North Queensland. He is a bald ordinary-looking man of who should be in his Fifties, even if he wasn't. He has an average journalist's beer belly – maybe even an average tribe's belly! -- and his dress and demeanor would smack of irreverence if he didn't appear so poorly representative of his black, of his white, side of him. His middle finger has always been too much in the air.

ACTOR 2
doubles as:
> **DEE** -- his twenty-one-year-old daughter in her two manifestations... the slovenly Scottish caricature to whom seeing him after 19 years is quite enough, and the sassy, smart and loving daughter who acts just as he imagines she lovingly would; and
> **MURIEL** – the Bench is more of a sexual work bench to her; a fine and honed woman of massive accomplishments and massive appetites, with a wit that has run through at least four husbands; she would never pretend it was intended to.

ACTOR 3
plays the lead glamorous, spirited roles of:
> **ALI** -- Rinner's first wife; crystal shining and beautiful who was just made for minks but intelligent enough to know it; and:

CINNAMON BROWN -- his 'Marlene Dietrich' obsession of anything-but Aboriginal stereotype; the curves she has always see daylight but, even so, she doesn't know what to do.

ACTOR 4:
SHEM – Cinnamon Brown's brother; his people leader-of-the-chin, their chief jaw jutter; learning to fake it when giving the fake back to the fake.

WEYDOM -- the Interpol agent ludicrously moonlighting as a State Prosecutor. He has the shark's feeding frenzy to go with what is described as the 'black blank eyes'; and

HUKKA -- the Amsterdam hotel's general hand; a Maori who would have joined any one of the refugee waves out of the Middle East merely because it would allow him to jump fences; probably working illegally but that's okay for a main-chancer.

ACTOR 5:
MAIYAH – the Amsterdam hotel's receptionist. She is a small dark shrewish Eurasian woman of Batavian-Chinese immigrant stock; if anyone is going to be a Javanese princess she'll tell you it should be her and 'no room' about it; and

RECEPTIONIST -- at the Sydney hotel, the booking register of which is entirely at her whim, or she'd kick you in the kkk-nackers; bad wig, worse broom cupboard.

Note for the character of Cinnamon Brown.
She has two stage impersonations as part of her act… Marlene Dietrich and Billie 'Lady Day' Holliday. Only Dietrich's 'Falling In Love Again' is given in the script here, but what songs and from which singer is up to the actor's voice strength and/or the directorial mood.

4

The Setting

The play is set in 'landscapes' of – mainly evoked – a bare-arsed apartment in Sydney which will ooze faded gentility, and the foyer of a small period-piece hotel in Amsterdam whose only note is that Marlene Dietrich and/or Mata Hari once stayed there, depending to whom you speak and on what day you do so.

More 'landscapes', however, are alluded to by extensive use of moderate spotlighting demanding subtle shades and timings of illumination.

Even with the Sydney apartment and the hotel foyers, there should be no need to light up a 'whole setting'. Props are better shadowed is possible. Certainly, no setting or prop is *not* instantly moveable from audience focus.

The tenure of the spotlighting underpins the whole play. As such… as a manifestation of Rinner's imagination… it is undoubtedly the mainstay of the performance.

NOTE: while he is obviously using the phone, RINNER is simply talking to the audience as if they were on the other end of the line.

Act 1
1.

(A darkened stage. A burglar alarm is ringing.

Eventually RINNER is lit from behind, as though he has just entered. He stands silhouetted for a long moment, looking confused and sick and sorry.

Then, while he stands there 'within' the noise of the alarm, he gradually sinks to his knees.

Even when the alarm stops, he stays down there on his hands and knees. But he can at least summon up the energy to mouth silent abuse up at the alarm.

General lighting comes up to show a striped-bare apartment in Sydney, that basically only has a wheelchair at back and an ornate wall mirror. In the centre of the floor there is a mobile phone on its charging cradle. It is more of a symbol than a prop. This he talks into either close up nor afar without having to lift it; its 'conference' mode is obviously on.

A dim spotlight emerges on the wheelchair at the back wall to slowly give it added emphasis, if only blurrily. We see that someone sits in silhouette. From this or back into this, most of the women will emerge or seem to sink back. It is certainly a presence that bears on him throughout.

Just now he crawls towards the phone, and lays down beside it.

When he recovers enough to stand on his feet, the alarm starts up again. He snaps his finger into the air. The alarm stops immediately.)

RINNER: Sometimes that works.

(which circumstantially keys on a banging on the wall from a neighbour. He shouts back)

RINNER: Hey, I'm trying to talk to a mirror here!

(This effort of shouting has a coughing-fit effect on him, but at least stops the banging)

RINNER: He doesn't know there's any mirror in here, but he falls for it every time. Dope.
   (adds to no one in particular)
What do you do when you find them dead?

(He manages to rise unsteadily, delivers into space that could be phone, could be audience)

RINNER: Whatever you do, don't ask me what I'm doing down here on my hands and knees... I only wanted to get down the street and pick up a packet of fags. I picked a butt I liked, ha ha. But I leave my keys inside here, don't I? So I think I might as well go down the boozer for a bit in the meantime. But when I get out to the car I've locked the keys inside there too. So when the NRMA arrives I try explaining I've left my keys in the boot not the car. They say they don't do boots. Get a shoe horn. Funny guy I say. He says, hey it's a boot why dontcha put a sock in it. Nice'n'choice. So I can't get in my car and can't get back into here.
   (pauses for another coughing spasm hurting his chest)
Okay, about the master key, I get up to the Body Corporate's guy's place and his missus answers the door. She says the Body Corporate guy's been waiting for me, where've I been? She says follow me. I follow. We get inside and there's Fatso sitting on the sofa and he's got his shirt and tie on alright, but no trousers. These old Y front and his john's hanging out and his hands resting on his lap covering up his old fellah which must have been the last thing he was tugging. Also, what could be worse was he's there with one black sock on one foot and one white sock on the other.
   (pause)

8

I blame that bloody alarm of mine. What I want to know is what's the most embarrassing... the yankery or the mismatching socks? And what do you do when you find them like that? You know what? I've just about had it.

(After hesitation, he adds, again to no one in particular)

RINNER: You heard the one about talking to a mirror?

(He goes over to the wall mirror and stares into it.

What he sees is obviously not even impressive to himself. Still, it is with an effort that he turns away and returns to the phone area. The banging on the wall starts up again. He responds calmly and strangely matter-of-factly:)

RINNER: Just ... Let me get on with this, 'kay?

(He shuffles towards the phone again, and continues his conversation 'into' it, even though – and throughout – he talks directly to the audience as though they were compositely on the other end as his daughter)

RINNER: Little girlie, whatever you do don't ask me what I 'm doing down here on my hands and knees. Like a bouncing ball, it's just the...you know... down swing.
  (stops to control more coughing, before suddenly bursting out with:)
Oh, God, I was so in love with your mother!
  (and)
I know, I know. She's yours as much as mine. Ali, our Ali. So... you've never asked: did your mother and I do it often? Oh, often, often. Beautifully, beautifully. In this I was privileged to swish and sway. Dear thing of her... mucking around washing my feet that time by licking her dear hands and, oh, slowly, in shine, looking up purring...

(As ALI comes up from the wheelchair and into her own spotlight where she kneels to continue his thought)

9

ALI: (very simply) I am, hon, wonderfully pregnant.

RINNER: Ah, Ali, Ali. Be crass. I need crass.

ALI: I can't sleep, hon, and I thought since you left me and baby whosies up here alone, why should you sleep down there in Sydney? So, because I love and miss you, why don't you just talk really dirty to me?'

RINNER: Ali, my Ali… I knew you'd know and ring. I'm going about court today 'I was brilliant' and you're dialing, right, my love? I'm going 'in court today' and you're dialing, right? I'm going 'wasn't I ever' and your lovely kisses already winging my way.

ALI: Dad says it's really pouring there.

RINNER: It hasn't seen rain here since Jesus got his feet wet.

ALI SILHOUETTE: You know Daddy. He thinks minks.

RINNER: He thinks what?

ALI: He thinks minks. Hon, there's a snake in the house.

RINNER: I hate snakes! Anyway who was that answered?

ALI: (ghostly giggle) Freddie from next door.

RINNER: He's not from next door; he's coming from my phone in my living room.

ALI: Silly. He's here getting the snake.

RINNER: I said I hate snakes!

ALI: Don't worry. It's in the roof and it's harmless.

RINNER: That snake burrowing away in his Y-fronts ain't! That bugger's a registered wife offender.

10

ALI: *(teasingly)* Why don't you ring me later and tell me all about that?

RINNER: Ah, crass.

ALI: Silly. Hon, I'd better go so I can ring Dad and Mum and tell her it isn't raining wherever you are there so she doesn't get too worried about the weather in the Holy Land just because Sunday's coming. Love tickle tickle...

> *(with big smacky kisses she starts to fade)*

RINNER: Don't go!

ALI: Okay.

RINNER: Babe, I wanted to tell you to forget about all this impotence talk stuff that jumped me after you told me you were preggers. Lay out mucho towels and jelly mixes by the side of the bed. The trial over in a few days and I'm coming home for the splash-down. Ali, my Ali...

ALI: Tell Dad and Mum I'll see them next week, if I forget to tell them tonight when she rings. I have to come down and get my little minks out of storage for their brush down. It's their three-months' walkies.

RINNER: Ali, we live in the tropics.

ALI: So did those lovely pelts once, hon.

RINNER: *(chortling)* Crass. My Ali.

> *(ALI fades, 'goes back' to wheelchair*
>
> *RINNER is left terribly alone)*

RINNER: Did I blink or something? Bloody long blink if I did. More of a blinkdom. Yes, little girlie, I was saying about...

what?; you remember?... well, I was locked out of this bloody apartment. So I get up to the Body Corporate's guy's place and his missus answers the door. She says you, and I say yes me, and she says he's been waiting for me for ages, where've I been? She says follow me. I follow. We get inside and there's Fatso sitting on the sofa and he's got his shirt and tie on alright, but no trousers. His john's hanging out and his hands resting on his lap covering up his old fellah which must have been the last thing he was tugging. Also, what could be worse was he's there with one black sock on one foot and one white sock on the other.

(*pause*)

What I want to know is what's the most embarrassing... the yankery or the mismatching socks? And what do you do when you find them like that? Also and so help me, I reckon if I hadn't locked myself out, she would never have found him like that. I've been a big help, she said.

> (*He leaves the phone, then slowly gets over to look in the mirror again, examines the lines around his eyes, his teeth, his hair, his tongue. He seems to have another spasm of chest pain before he turns back into the room again*)

RINNER: No, stugger it, I'm not waiting until next week...!

> (*He extracts an airmail letter from his pocket, reads a phone number and goes back and dials STD... again it is more of a conversation with the audience rather than someone in Amsterdam. By the time it is answered he is well down stage, almost in the audience's lap and speaking directly to them:*)

RINNER: Hello! Is that...
    (*gets cut off, redials irritably*)
Kindly don't come that again. Dee Rinner, please. *Dee Rinner*. Hey, look, you speak English? No, I'm speaking English! No, I don't speak Dutch. Is there...
    (*has to listen again*)
No, I don't speak Syrian. Sorry, no Sudanese Arabic either. Look, Dee Rinner there? Who? No, shissake, I'm not speaking Indonesian. It's Australian. Something similar, okay, okay. What?

Look, listen... no, I'm not ringing from the Indonesian authorities about your complaint concerning how badly the Dutch nation's treating you.

(*to audience*)

So help me the conversation was going like this.

(*then back, lying like a dog, 'into' phone*)

Me? You serious? Well, I might be a dad, but sprightly like you wouldn't guess. Thick black on top, not a jungle clearing in sight. Tall, some say debonair but I usually demur. I'm the type for which it's a shame video phones haven't come in too much yet, say so m'self. Married, me? No, no; only a few bits hanging off me. So, now that you have me down to a T, d'think my daughter's coming to the phone? Sure, I'll hang on. Why not it's been nineteen years, so what's a minute or two between friends? Sure I mean you and me are friends.

(*to audience*)

I mean we had to be, right? Would we be having moonlight dinners if we weren't, ha ha?

(*Equivalently, he covers the mike attached to his shirt front, holds his head in his hands to control his frustration, then turns back to the mobile to try again*)

RINNER: Whazzat? Sure you'd fit in in Australia. Yes, you'd be allowed to divorce me if you wanted to. No, Australia's farther away from Austria than Rio.

(*But gives it up anyway. He lies back on the floor by the phone... obviously now a familiar place for him*)

RINNER: (*into air*) Moonlight dinners with some dusky voiced Asian? Yeah, I should be so lucky to still be awake that late.

(*he is slowing down again*)

Still there, little girlie? Of course you're still there. Anyway, I can tell you in all honesty, there was no way I could ever say to your mother that no male in the Rinner side has ever survived the next pregnancy. I mean, lying there avoiding the prospect of sex with our Ali thinking about how wonderful sex with her was. Stuff me, sorry, but what can you say about a man who uses wire wool on our tongue in the shower? This is Dad here.

13

(can't, now, keep eyes open)
Pardonnez, little girl, maybe just a little shut-eye…

(In tune with his eye lids, there is a slow blackout)

2.

(Forty winks later. A general 'sleepy' haze of a lighting effect comes over the apartment. RINNER is half awake.

ALI emerges back out from the wheelchair. She is joined by PA, her father, who remains off to the side)

RINNER: (not real) What's he doing here? He should be preparing his leg for the next lamp pole...
   (even so, dreamily submissive)
... Sir.

PA: Dag wouldn't know shit from sugar.

RINNER: Could've got a taxi. Sir.

PA: The dag'd be lucky. Sydney's taxis're on strike.

RINNER: Hired a car, could have. Sir.

PA: Dag'd be lucky. Petrol on strike.

RINNER: Hopped a train.

PA: They're out with the Sydney buses. Talk about a dag.

RINNER: Sir, these feet have jump-starts.

PA: Dag thinks he's too good for the Maserati.

ALI: I'm driving!

RINNER: Sir, a night patrol with loss of life would be safer!
Drop me off at the Milson Hotel? Alive?

PA: Oughta drop the dag off where he shoulda been instead of
marrying my little girl... at the bottom of Sydney Harbour.
Wouldn't know his slvong from his slvshort. Hey, Dag, what's a
slvong? No? Dag. Well, what's a slvshort?
   (snorts derision at surly silence)
Dag from Dagestan.

   (He 'disappears'. RINNER drops 'back' with relief)

RINNER: You see the kids past their mums and dads? Frag-
meant suicide bomber becomes spineless, blows his cover over
alert guard. Frag-meant man shown to be a man of many parts.
(shouts) Ali?!

ALI: Ssh. Drop off...

RINNER: Or are we blowing bubbles?

ALI: Drop off now...

   *(He does so. She 'fades' back to wheelchair, while the
   RECEPTIONIST at the Milson – she is MAI YAH without
   the Chinese/Javanese pidgin accent to come and with a
   badly-fitting nylon wig – appears leeringly)*

RECEPTIONIST: *(cheshire grin)* Help you?

RINNER: Not with that nightmare of a wig.

RECEPTIONIST: Then wake up. Name, other than Rinner?

RINNER: Why other than Rinner?

RECEPTIONIST: Sorry, full up. Stiff stuff of the Chrissie turkey.

15

RINNER: I booked. I got on that thing there. That's called a telephone.

RECEPTIONIST: Did I say sorry or didn't I bother? Only booking in name of Rinner is from Cairns.

RINNER: I'm Rinner from Cairns.

RECEPTIONIST: Well, the other Rinner from Cairns, who is a real gentleman, made a booking, or didn't I say?

RINNER: There is no other Rinner from Cairns other than my wife!

RECEPTIONIST: We would need some form of written proof about that.

RINNER: They can't write in Cairns!

RECEPTIONIST: That's a shame in this day and age.

RINNER: Where are we? Darkest Africa? I've been all over Africa. They can read and write in Africa!

RECEPTIONIST: Would this man kindly stop looking down my blouse?

RINNER: I wasn't. Well, I was. But that's not the point.

RECEPTIONIST: If you must know, Mr Rinner from Cairns happens to be a real gentleman calling himself Mr Rinner from Afghanistan.

RINNER: They don't have Rinner in Afghanistan, except me, and I departed with the one-millionth child casualty under 10 years ago!

RECEPTIONIST: There's no need to fly off the handle. Unless you want a kick in the camels.

RINNER: I only want a room.

RECEPTIONIST: *(primly)* I can only give you a kick in the camels.
(one breath again, peering at terminal)
Well, we might have one right at the end of the top floor. It's a broom cupboard. It's got a view. If you're not fussy about not having a bathroom or a bed. And I don't know what you'd do with your clothes. I think Housekeeping could manage a nail in the door but don't tell Management I said that. I see it's already got a camp stretcher. Folded up. The door can be opened while it remains so which is quite good for a broom cupboard.

RINNER: (into air) A small thing like five, say, maybe four-and-a-half star treatment, little girlie. I mean, how petty can the court system of Australia get?
(then back 'down' to receptionist)
Expert witnesses don't fall out of trees, you know.

RECEPTIONIST: *(*agreeing*)* Not on toast, they don't.
(then)
Well?

RINNER: Well, what?

RECEPTIONIST: What do I put you down as?

RINNER: Put me down as Rinner, man from UNICEF not-so-long-ago.

RECEPTIONIST: How long ago?

RINNER: I still can't forget it.

RECEPTIONIST: (fading) Okay, you deserve a favour. You've got the broom cupboard. Do I put you down as folding up your own cot in the mornings or Housekeeping's gotta force the door to see if it's you blocking the door? Just a reminder to all our clients: if you call Milson's home, we reserve the right to sue you.

(RINNER is left alone. But he is at least now fully awake again. He returns to his phone call)

RINNER: Little girl, still there? Of course, of course.
  (and simply addresses the audience)
You would've wanted to ask before why I was off in Sydney and your mother left up in Cairns. Bit of a long story I can expand on next week. In a nutshell, though, a few years after the Childrens Fund I went to the Age's shigger of an editor and said I'd like to be a travel writer covering places where there's no kids getting blown to pieces and he said okay the only place he knew on earth like that was Cairns but only because the Australian census hasn't caught up with Cairns yet. I said hey that's a bit rough on my home town and he said okay scrub that; you're going up there because it's thousands of clicks away. So, having your mother with her delicious pretensions on accounta her money and loverly, lubberly crassness, had to make me the instant expert on the local Yirrgandjis, right? Me being half-half didn't hurt, of course. So, when Shem… her brother… and don't ask me who 'her' is, okay?; they say bytes can still melt under the hottest of hickeys, 'kay?… so when that Shem propels that Greenie out of one of the hardwoods the Greenie's protesting about into the gorge below by agency of a length of bamboo, guess who become The Expert Witness at the murder trial moved down here to Sydney? You point and I'll whistle.

    (During this, JUDGE MURIEL has 'emerged' from the wheelchair while SHEM and WEYDOM emerge into a lit area opposite. She is crudely attired as a sitting judge; SHEM wears an identifying Aboriginal Land Rights bandanna. Weydom has on a corny sleuth's trench coat and large-brimmed hat. The Judge sits, and the men stand as defendant and State prosecutor respectively)

RINNER: The trouble, little girlie, is I've always been so circumstantially impotent.
  (Sickly, RINNER begins to wave his arms like waving seaweed)
Sea wallows yet still the land mines unerring. What a dummy your father is to our worst nature!

18

(He turns to a very amused JUDGE MURIEL and 'enters' into the first court scene)

RINNER: Muriel?

MURIEL: Darling Rinny, if I don't still carry your hickey!

RINNER: Where'd Wardrobe dig up that moth-eaten get-up?

MURIEL: *(at court)* Let it be put on record I know the expert witness but that has never stopped me, ha ha.
  (command)
All park khyber passes!

(which is the cue for SHEM to pipe up:)

SHEM: I don't no way cognify this fucking court!

MURIEL: That's funny. I was here yesterday, and I'm positive I *cognified* you.

SHEM: I got my own cognify. I don't give a root what your white slitbums cognify!

(Prosecutor WEYDOM takes over)

WEYDOM: Are you Pieter Garel Rinner, expert witness?

RINNER: *(nodding)* Embedded once.

MURIEL: (lewdly) I can vouch for that. Move it on.

WEYDOM: What unit were you embedded in?

RINNER: They didn't give me a unit. They gave me a broom cupboard. A stain on the court system, Judge!

WEYDOM: I didn't ask if you'd been embedded, Mr Rinner.

RINNER: Jesus, fair go, Judge.

19

MURIEL: Call me Your Honour or no more embedding me for you, Rinny you naughty-but-nice cunny chaser from Cairns, you.

RINNER: It's better than chasing cars, Your H.

MURIEL: Has the expert witness forgotten his shoes?

RINNER: (painfully inept) They seemed to fly off and never come back, Your Honour, but having said that, in my expert-witness capacity, I'd have to admit I'm not so sure they did so voluntarily.

MURIEL: Talking of which in a not way, would you like to reserve the court's needle and thread for your socks or am I just fluffy in bed?

RINNER: (scorn at WEYDOM) Thought I'd kick off with a small dissertation about Australia's policy on war victims, Your Honour.

MURIEL: I prefer us staying with your socks. The prosecutor should proceed by getting his eyes off the witness's socks before potatoes start growing between his toes too.

WEYDOM: Mr Rinner, in your expert opinion, do you stand by your previous expert advice that a single hotel... say, any one pub in the whole of Far North Queensland... openly pursuing an illegal policy of not serving people of Aboriginal descent on the feeble excuse they have no money... that that pub could have been a major contributing factor in the Defendant's murderous behaviour?

RINNER: In my opinion?

WEYDOM: In your "expert" opinion, Mr Rinner.

RINNER: No.

WEYDOM: That so? Why have you changed your mind since you last took the oath?

RINNER: In my opinion?

WEYDOM: In your expert opinion, Mr Rinner.

RINNER: No.

WEYDOM: But do you stand by your statement that, and I quote…
   (reads from court records)
'the questions of historical culpability, the causative effects of Aboriginal actions, are *sine qua non* to certain cynosural acts of certain black persons in or out of the 'ordinary' criminal realm of acts such as acts of logging tied to acts of cantankerised violence or of the calumny of someone of the Green Australia party persuasion being dislodged out of a tree over a gorge by an extent of bamboo?'

RINNER: Who said that?

WEYDOM: You did, Mr Rinner.

RINNER: Well, a man's entitled to an expert opinion.

WEYDOM: Knock it off! Yesterday you told this mob here that turfing the defendant out of any pub, or any public dunny like, was the inevitable prelude to the Defendant's social shortcomings but not necessarily violence like being prodded out of a tree with parking rights belonging to no tribe or person. Did you or did you not say that?

RINNER: In my opinion?

WEYDOM: In your expert opinion, Mr Rinner.

RINNER: Yes.

WEYDOM: And do you still get off with:

(reads)

'Questions of historical culpability in the coming of the white man have a great bearing on acts of certain black persons, whether these acts of violence be against trees or people sitting in trees?'

RINNER: In my opinion, allowing that I haven't really had a good think about it…?

WEYDOM: Yes.

RINNER: Then yes.

WEYDOM: Have you or have you not stated "No" to those same questions earlier?

RINNER: In my expert opinion?

WEYDOM: In your expert opinion, please.

RINNER: I'd have to take a stab at yes and no, providing I said it. All I can say is: I certainly deny saying it otherwise.

WEYDOM: An answer, please, Mr Rinner.

RINNER: I'll certainly give an expert witness's opinion as to some thought on the matter, Your Honour.
  (leans over for whisper)
How much time have I got, Muriel?

JUDGE MURIEL: I think the witness may step down.

RINNER: Well, I don't know about that, Your Honour. I really only came upon the murder scene the moment it all happened. One minute you're there, the next accusations are flying like some poor Greenie falling out of a tree and, stiff cheese, over into a gorge, like. I mean, nobody asks are these your socks and shoes or do we all say sayonara?

> *(MURIEL and the court scene fade… she back into the wheelchair.*

Blackout.

Near-instantaneous lighting back on RINNER in bare apartment. He is at the mirror, can finally pull himself away to:)

RINNER: Little girlie, I was pretty pleased by the expert way that had turned out.

(There is a blackout as quick as a wink)

3.

(Momentarily, lighting back on him. It blinks as he blinks before:)

RINNER: The land mines unerring, yes. In this sea, this sea.
   (stops, thinking she saw him give an expression)
What am I talking about 'in this sea, this sea'? They'll find me with one white sock on and one black sock on soon.
   (then)
It's not Ali. No, it definitely isn't your dear mother I feel coming on.   Close your ears. Go and make tea or something.
   (shudders with pleasure)
No, no. It was… It was…
   (and)
It was just *her*, don't you see?, and a weak… and a weak… and a weak man, don't you see?...

   (CINNAMON BROWN emerges from the wheelchair. She is on the steps of the courthouse, is evidently talking to a gaggle of print and media reporters while backing him up against the wall.

   She is more than a little gaudy, baubled and bangled and painted, heavy eye-liner, but with a Marlene Dietrich

23

vaudeville top hat and showing, a la Dietrich, more than a hint of thigh and black net stocking. When she swears she uses the words deliberately.

Mesmerically, he rises to her, does a demeaning cobra-like dance before her)

CINNAMON BROWN: (to throng) Call that fugging farce a fugging trial?

RINNER: (whispered and desperate aside) She still causes me pain in this sea, this sea... whisky washing down us in a broom cupboard at the Milson Hotel, and slow-drawn...

CINNAMON: *(*to some reporter*)* To answer your numb-arse question...I'm the defendant's sister, never mind who the fug I am. And don't you go asking me why that shithead of a judge's threatening me with contempt of court. Numb-arsed if I know. I'm just a nice working gal from Cairns butting into his life, but don't ask me who 'his' is, though I'm pretty sure it's my butt. All I know is he's working against me.

RINNER: *(sudden succubus, miming wriggling hips against her:) Who's Outback? She is great out back! She'd be a silky road root! Where's she? Them there those nails filed on no Mt Lumley nor beetle-crushers grating on a Cape Trib cairn, two fruity piles behind. Cinnamon! Name's the colour of! All tropical lush, all gush, all bum's rush. Brown! Brown as a berry! Drown is the Djirrandji mob around Cairns! You watch her voice hanging in the sung coral night... where am I?... throaty as the bubbling of the dry-throat of the coolabah... Hindmostly rocky or just Cairns-y? Where, where? Flesh press as the chocolate evening sure to lushly be. She is as they are the people of the vast tropics great leaf covering her fronds at night!...*

CINNAMON: Hey, stow it back there!
    (answering question again)
How's my little brother taking it? Frig off! What fug of a ding-a-ling asked that?

24

RINNER: Miss Brown, how is your brother taking it?

CINNAMON: My poor brother Shem's had a bomb put under him by way of wrongful encapturement. He's fugging shattered and torturing himself.

RINNER: What about the deceased victim, Miss Brown?

CINNAMON: How do I know? Maybe he's shattered, too, so what? This is all a bum's wrap.

RINNER: *(in musth derangement)* A NICE BUM! A WONDERFUL WRAP OF HER HUNKERS! FRAG-MEANT MAN GOT UPROOTED, CAME DOWN FROM A REAL HIGH!
   (then madly backing her up)
This is a shagging disgrace! As an expert I ought to know!

CINNAMON: To answer your shitty question...I'm the wrongly accused's sister, never mind who the fug I am. You kidding me? I'm an artiste at La Bumba. Catch the show and brighten your sorry little life, whitie. And they gotta quit him. No fugging lesser charge of frigging manslaughter or something. What red-blooded Aboriginal man can live with a piss weak thing like manslaughter and look his mates in the eye? Always trying to take away our dignity.
   (grossly backs into RINNER)
Bump, bump.
   (over shoulder to him but surprisingly softly)
Ssh, babe, ssh.

   (She leaves him, re-emerges into the wheelchair.

   He moves back over to the mirror and into it:)

RINNER: Did anyone tell you about the one about talking to a mirror?

   (For a moment that hangs in the air like it did the last time he said it. But then, as MURIEL re-emerges from the

25

wheelchair, he speaks to her via her reflection in the mirror.)

RINNER: What about you, Judge? You heard the one about talking to a mirror? I bet you have. I mean, do any of us shine lights that aren't reflections? How many times did I shine a light in little eyes, do you think?

(she has settled back at the intimation of her desk in her chambers, lights up a cheroot, put her feet up on the desk)

MURIEL: How many, Rinny?

RINNER: Little eyes? Little she eyes? Little he eyes? Both I guess. Oh, many, many, Muriel J. Hello, you go. Hello in there? Oh.
  (has to stop)
You know, the Childrens Fund said it's okay, it's not the soul sinking. It's just the eye shrinking back into the socket. It's just you being out in the field. I think it's the soul sinking.

MURIEL: I think so too.

RINNER: (nods thanks, then:) Nice high heels thrown ponst your desk, Judge. Mind if I slide digit up thigh?

MURIEL: Rinny, the latest American surge up in Darwin tried and was found wanting. Now, you naughty fragment of a man you, I'd like to think we can be finished by Friday arvo, what think?

RINNER: My expert-witness opinion, Judge?

MURIEL: Your expert-witness opinion, Mr Rinner.

RINNER: Yes and no, unless that's not the answer you're looking for.

MURIEL: I like to think I could avoid mentioning you as an absolute bloody disgrace in my summary. What do you think there, my cluck?'

RINNER: In my expert opinion, Your Huggable?

MURIEL: In your expert opinion, yes, while your tongue is looking so itchy.

RINNER: I never said one way or the other. If I did, I certainly deny saying it, Your Ogle-able.

MURIEL: Call me Muriel or put your pants back on. The thing being I'd like to get this trial over with by Friday because I'm not allowed to fraternise with you as a witness and so I won't be able to go to the Black and White Ball.

RINNER: I'm shocked, Your Prominence-in-parts. I'm married.

MURIEL: Not that way, goose. Ali's got a nice Snow Leopard mink I'm desperate to borrow and trot along to the white part of that ball.

RINNER: Snow leopards are an endangered species, Muriel!

MURIEL: Don't you think your little Ali and I know that? I'm going to wear its label on the outside so everybody else knows it too. So... by Friday?

RINNER: Well, I don't know, Your Oompfable.

MURIEL: What if I tone down my ridicule of your performance and only mention it in passing?

RINNER: How much in passing, Your Thighsome?

MURIEL: A shoot-through on the inside kind of passing. Zip.

RINNER: Zip, Your Down-zippership?

MURIEL: Zip. So what's our verdict on Mr Shem Whosit?

RINNER: Hang him by the neck, Your Heavenly-gatedom?

27

MURIEL: No no no. I thought a little manslaughter with empho on mitigating circs. Everybody gets to be happy with manslaughter. Fall back on it often. So... what think or do I have to remove my stilettos before your naked eyes?

RINNER: What think about what, Your Hockness?'

MURIEL: That as an expert witness you're a rutting insult to our legal history but that doesn't get mentioned outside our soiled sheets, ha ha.

(WEYDOM emerges in his own lighting, while they:)

RINNER: Manslaughter does have a nice ring to it, Your Murielship.

MURIEL: Call me Your Honour or don't throw your leg over me again, ha ha. So... Mr Shem Whosit is a fortunate young man to have an expert witness like you in his corner, Mr Rinner.

RINNER: That it, Your Honour-it-if-asked?

MURIEL: We'll see each other at the Ball but you can't touch, yep.

(They go to leave off from one another, but WEYDOM jumps in)

WEYDOM: Hold it right there!

(RINNER takes one look at him and goes to bolt)

WEYDOM: Not so fast!

(RINNER stops, turns back)

RINNER: I'm only stopping because nobody says 'Not so fast' anymore.

WEYDOM: In Interpol we do. It's our motto.

(RINNER swings away to speak as in a phone call but to the audience again)

RINNER: Little girlie, so now you know why I could well be tinkling you from a broom cupboard and going from too many little legs thin as matchsticks and nobbly and ungainly to a Judge's chambers' gams all very toothsome'n'gainly. Say it's the varied life your father has led. Why need one follow the swishing burqa when one has gently-swaging judges in our land?

(He turns back to the waiting WEYDOM)

RINNER: Say it again.

WEYDOM: Not so fast!

RINNER: There, you've said it again.

WEYDOM: I did not.

RINNER: You did.

WEYDOM: If you so smart why are you still going to get on that flight to Indonesia knowing I'm dobbing you in for the packet you're carrying to the Indonesians?

RINNER: (stopping, thinking) I know *you* won't arrest me now on a little possession because you want to give the Indos's death sentence a leg-up, right?

WEYDOM: Practise makes perfect. But not so fast.

RINNER: Stop saying that!
  (and then outcry)
THEY SHOOT YOU DEADER'N A DOORNAIL THERE!

(Blackout.

In the interim, for the first time we hear it, CINNAMON singing 'Falling In Love Again' in mimic of Marlene Dietrich.)

4.

(Lighting up on a scene that has a distinct dreamy pace to it.

CINNAMON is doing her Marlene Dietrich routine. She sits reverse-astride a simple bentwood chair, her legs wide apart but tantalisingly covered, of course, by the back of the chair.

RINNER is in stupor on presumably the stage floor looking up at her, mouth agape, in her thrall. She must look colossal to him. Her head is backlit to silhouette. She could be the reincarnated Kali with her huge show-time headdress reaching out into the universe above him; her barely-covered bauble'n'bangle'n'beads body monumental. It is the seventh of heaven, the glow of All-gosh.

Her voice is husky and grainy, smoke-ridden:
Falling in love again
What I am to do...?
What're I to do;
I can't help it.

She finishes her routine, looks down over back of chair, down to RINNER)

CINNAMON: (to SHEM) Our expert witness!

SHEM: Expert witless! Witless! A slob!

CINNAMON: A-slobber?

(RINNER laughs up at her imbecilely. He is obviously worse for wear)

CINNAMON: Our Ex-ness. Sir Ex-ness!

RINNER: (blinded, thick-tongued) How do? Me fragment and frag meant blows you back where you belong.

CINNAMON: I back into you again, you gonna go all pelvis on me again, Sir Ex-ness?

RINNER: Not saying! I'll say!

CINNAMON: That right, Sir Ex-ness?

RINNER: (trying to get in good with brother) Frag 'em all, Shem! Shame! What's a push-a-Greenie-outa-the-tree?

(Whereupon she imperiously beckons him to follow. In spotlight and drumroll, he follows in her striding wake obviously for at least one complete circle)

CINNAMON: Come

RINNER: Coming.

CINNAMON: Come.

RINNER: Coming.

(They return to where they were. She pulls his face into the darkness, obviously pressing it against her pelvis.

Both he and she freeze in that position for too long, as though his brain has stopped working. Finally, it seems to get working again:)

RINNER: Quincy breath fanned down sweet fandango.

31

SHEM: Hey, the cocklehead's got white stuff coming out of his temple.

RINNER: ShemShame, haven't I been known as Elephant Head in my time! Never mind the ichors!

CINNAMON: Sir Ex-ness, like my voice?

RINNER: Like? Tis a wormhole of wonders a-suckle!

SHEM: *(suspicious)* What's doing, Witless?

RINNER: Brudda Shem! She knows me, Shame Less! I met her behind a brush with each other on the courthouse steps, so you can hold up on the detonator, ha ha.

SHEM: (warning) No fiddling up my sis, Witless.

RINNER: (playing the fool) I am the Rin what stands on the Rinner of the world, ShameShem! I am a fragment named Frag! Boom, boom! Frag-meant arms went up and jaws dropped! Frag-meant eye drops out! Frag-meant some parts of a man became his sum parts! Frag-meant off the top of your head! See?

CINNAMON: Sir Ex-ness, sounds to me like you've got the impotents.

RINNER: Blame my Ali, my lov'liest of All-ests, cream bun in creamy oven-y lovel-y getting but.

CINNAMON: Bye, Sir Ex-ness.

RINNER: By Sir Ex-ness who?

   (Blackout)

5.

*(Lighting back on lone RINNER. He is holding his head.
After last scene, this could be from a hangover. He lays
blessedly down by the phone, has to wind up from a slow,
tortured beginning... as he does so he actually crawls to
front stage to the audience:)*

RINNER: You see, little girlie, what I think is there wouldn't be
any dying all around if there weren't any human beings all around.
No wonder the DNA strand has so many twists to it.
   (and)
Is that you breathing, my Dee, my little-y? Think you could do it
a bit less heavily? That's a ha ha. But you see I know it's not the
best for a father to have to say this to his little missing girl, but it
hasn't helped any that I've always looked drunk in my life. You
should hear this mirror here complain how it always has to look
back at me so shikkered.

   *(He dozes off for a few seconds, but then jerks awake with,
   obviously, a frightening image)*

RINNER: *It will never go away, will it?!*
   (then)
Little girlie, watch out for the eye as shutter-byes. They were
videoing and I didn't know it. It was a petrol station they had
bombed, next to a playground.
   (painfully)
Next to a playground. Next to a playground. I don't know what
goes with every time *I* look down I see a little movement; I see a
little life. How can't you pick the child up and run? Above the
petrol shed women were throwing their babies out of the windows
amongst the flames. It was raining babies and I looked and I saw
the little one smoking away in my arms. 'I'm sick of this fucking
bullshit!' Who shouted that?
   (and)
I don't even know how I got into this patrol vehicle. Australian
army. Good eggs. Googs. Googs. Good eggs, those, and I
shouted 'Go!' and they shouted back 'Where?' and I shouted 'I'll
know; just go!'. We passed a burning car upside down with a man

in the driver's seat waving about like he was trying to ward off flies. The child charring away in my arms. I shouted down next one to the hospital. Which one?, who shouted? I yelled, 'Left!' I meant right. I yelled 'Left!' when I know I wanted to yell 'Right!' *Honestly*! Little girlie…

(*struggles with*)

we got lost down left, stuck in traffic. We got caught down there in a jam. And we… you see… we couldn't get to hospital in near, near enough time.

Charred on my hands
I still have the bands

(*like a plainsong*)

Oh, little girlie, maybe you can tell me why I shouted left instead of what I meant, right.

(*and, ditto monotone*)

They took one look at me and said I must've been drunk. They did. They took one look at me and said I must've been drunk.

(For a moment he doesn't seem to know where to turn to. He sees the mirror, at least:)

RINNER: That's the other thing this mirror keeps complaining about… have to look at me with such dirty hands.

(Blackout)

6.

(Lighting back on RINNER at mirror.

Emerging from the wheelchair is the RECEPTIONIST)

RINNER: I know I'm miserable if it's you again.

RECEPTIONIST: They must think yours truly is a singing telegram.
Our Rin went to ground in the Afghan war
When they found him in near pieces

He expounded the thesis
He was even more fragmented than before.
  (chorus)
Oh, the head on his shoulders
Made such a lot of pearler boulders.

RINNER: Very funny.

RECEPTIONIST: I'm only here because I've been pushed into it.
Apparently someone has to tell you you're due at your inlaws for
lunch.
  (remembering what she has to say)
Oh, and they told me especially to add 'Y'dag'.

RINNER: (whine) That father-in-law wants to kill me at table
tennis.

RECEPTIONIST: You've had plenty of chances to get rid of him.

RINNER: I tried once. It was with a 12.7mm Accuracy
International AW50 Anti Materiel Rifle AMR the Childrens' Fund
issued for use in Ethopian kindergartens. It had blockbusting
projectiles but it got blocked in the mail, ha ha.
  (then high spirits)
Bring inlaws on!

RECEPTIONIST: Oh, and apparently you need to be reminded
how long you've been waiting for this moment. Whatareya?

RINNER: *(mock modesty)* In the boom-boom of things, tis but
fragments in time when two people passing in the night can be
said to exchange passing glances amongst other parts they were
once exclusively attached to.

RECEPTIONIST: I hope you know it doesn't get to have another
ending.

RINNER: Nothing improvises like an Improvised Explosive
Device, ha ha.

RECEPTIONIST: (unexplained warning) That's what you say. Like I said, pity it ain't for breakfast and they could have you on toast.

(and while she 'returns' to the wheelchair:)

RINNER: (after her) About that broom cupboard of yours, why don't you return that mop on your head to it?

(Inlaws PA and MA sniggeringly appear)

PA: Dag's gone all limp-dick on our little Ali.

MA: No male wedded to this family goes squidgy in this house! I just bought my little girl a maternity mink all the way from a family of little Siberian minks, thank you very much.

RINNER: Give them back! Ask any fragment in life you'd like as to what bits the fur flies from, and that's what I think anyway.

PA: Dag's sad sack's all shrivelled.

MA: *(calling and fading)* Rightio, it's on the table!

RINNER: It's not on the table! It's never on the fucking table!

PA: (cackling*)* Hey, Daggy, shake!

(Of course, RINNER falls for the old trick of offering his hand and having the old boy madly whip his away)

PA: *(*delighted, fading too*)* Dag'll never learn.

RINNER: (furiously shouts after them*)* There's nothing on the table because there's no fucking food and no fucking table! I'm not setting any table anymore and I'm not sitting there passing plates to the thousands of you buggers just because your daughter's the most wonderful together thing in the fragments of my time!

(He is left alone and feels it)

RINNER: *Hello?*
  (nothing)
It's like your average patrol coming across a bat cave. It might look nothing but you can see some shit's been going on, ha ha.
  (tries again)
YOO HOO?!

(PA and MA re-emerge with a folding table, set it up)

PA: Dag's going all racially little-girlsie.

RINNER: Sir and Madam, I know what it is. It's all this talk about impotence. It leaves a man vulnerable. It must be on show, flaccid-wise somehow – or else, and more's the like, Ali's put it out over the wires, as in her husband's meat is a jugged hare, but his jugular's easy meat. Nice going, Ali.

PA: Dag's chucking a shitty.

MA: Shitty livers ain't *in* in this family. They are *out.*

RINNER: Sir and Madam, the thing is, see, how can one's own beloved wife tell the world of one's impotents when she was the one who made one get her pregnant? Is that not a bit rough?
  (sickly sweet)
Hello, Mummy.

MA: *(*horrified*)* Hello.

RINNER: Have I told you about expert witness? Have I told you how it's taught me to kick Aussie arse?

MA: (miserably) No.

PA: Dag doesn't know his doosie from his humdinger.

RINNER: (at PA, deliberately childish) Kick, kick.

37

PA: (surly) 'Off, y'dag.

RINNER: (but now jaunty) Shall we be at nosh and toast our Ali?

(Grudgingly they sit. RINNER is now in high spirits to the phone)

RINNER: Little girlie, introducing your grandfather and grandmother, Sir and Ma Popsicle! What a well brow-knitted lot we are! I told them, I did, pass the shagging produce of Alsace for sampling before allowing the smoked Canadian salmon to be place before me, lemoned, I trusted, and garnished with fried Roquefort coated with cinnamon. Ere I tucked in, I reached for the Niersteiner to prepare the palate for the bouillabaisse that I would come to declare too salty. I expressed the thought that the Liebfraumilch might be a titch more refined than usual, but not much. I nudged Ma Popsicle to chop-chop with opening the Mateus and towards admitting her roast beef needed a fruitier burgundy to tempt its sauce, some crushed rose leaves to settle in its stuffing, a sprinkling of vanilla essence to free its potential and a soupcon of desiccated custard to invigorate its vegetables. I said looking around I could see there was glum pudding to come, and hoped that wouldn't be before the filet mignon or the porc filet which I expected to be filled with oysters marinated in beetroot. It was but regretfully I could only say so-so. I pointed out how the thriving family couldn't expect to continue its high profits unless it engaged me at its helm on high perks. Glum as glum could be, were they. The fish candies I thought also verging on the moderate; that the cleansing ale should have been Steinlager; but I kept the downgrading of the kitchen's stars within reasonable bounds.

(From brutish, teeth-showing revenge, he suddenly collapses to the floor when MA's phone rings.

She pulls it from her pocket, delightedly standing to answer it thinking it will be ALI)

MA: Ali... Darling!

38

(But it is obviously not ALI. She listens. Her body tightens. Then she collapses onto the floor beside RINNER.

PA gets 'moving' to take up the phone.

He too listens. He too collapses beside them.

RINNER can move his arms enough to prise the mobile away from PA and to listen himself. He lets the phone drop, collapses down beside them)

MA: *(*in trauma*)* You left her alone.

RINNER: Freddie said it was harmless!

MA: *You left her alone!*

RINNER: *They said it wasn't poisonous! They said watch out only for the unflailing minefields!*

(end Act 1)

Act 2
7.

(Lighting up on RINNER alone at the mirror. He is mumbling into it, but we cannot hear what he is saying. He is, and remains, totally grief-stricken for the duration of this Act; even when it looks like he is trying to be animated, it is with a distinct dull quality.

He turns back from the mirror, returns to the central phone. It lights up in a weird participation even as he approaches, sits beside it, and -- only eventually, and even then, only barely able to -- comes out with the first of:)

RINNER: Little girlie, tell your mother if you ever see her: to be honest, I wasn't really ever at my best.

(FREDDIE from Ali's next door appears, barely venturing on stage. He has a sheepish grin on his face which looks more like rictus:)

FREDDIE: It's Freddie. Next door, eh?

RINNER: (makes slithering movements with his hand) Bastard. Three guesses what this is?

FREDDIE: *(outcry) I don't know!*

RINNER: It's a snake, you drongo.
    (and)
If you had any decency you'd have dropped dead of idiocy.

FREDDIE: She said it was only a rat snake.

RINNER: No, she didn't.

FREDDIE: *(gut-wrench) Next day, I went to get my eyes tested!*
    (FREDDIE withdraws frightfully. RINNER groans, and:)
40

RINNER: (again) Little girlie, tell your mother if you ever see her: to be honest, I wasn't really ever at my best.

(Strains of Billie Holliday's 'I'll be Seeing You Again' by CINNAMON come over. He sways to it with that curious swaying-seaweed motions again.

While CINNAMON BROWN emerges slinkingly from the wheelchair, her brother SHEM appears opposite. He has an accompanying guitar over his shoulder but is incongruously dressed in dinner jacket and bowtie like a burlesque magician would be)

SHEM: Yo, Witless! Get your Cross-bred-arsed bum over here! Y'wanna share a suck-up, sniff sniff?
(He holds up his arm, palm outwards; blood drips down his hand)

SHEM: I'm trying to get my mojo back too, Witless. I'm tellingya keep out of them bar fights.

RINNER: ('what to do?') Fragment gets to play on one's nerves.

SHEM: Witless, you watch your slung arse or they'll slap a piss-weak manslaughter onya. Suspended, double the insult! Every bugger thinks you're piss weak. Hey, Witless! Join the band, man! Y'doan wanna join the band, joint-up the band, man!

RINNER: I can probably do that.

(By now, CINNAMON has come to him, looks down on him, but with much sympathy)

RINNER: (up at her; yet again) To be honest, I wasn't ever much at my best.

CINNAMON: Sir Ex-ness, crashed out down here in your own garage?

41

RINNER: Floored. Cinnamon.

CINNAMON: Thick-tongue, huh?

RINNER: A bit slopping, anyone lobbing?

> *(They are interrupted by loud radio programs and people crashing around 'upstairs')*

CINNAMON: It's what you get for standing outside of the club going to the people, 'Who's for rent-free?' You could've got us all killed in the stampede.

RINNER: Your mob?

CINNAMON: (meaning upstairs) All fifty or more.

RINNER: I look like in the mirror?

CINNAMON: I've got a sequin'd number that doesn't shimmer shake as much as you are.

RINNER: Can I help you before I slide off the earth?

CINNAMON: My crazy brother gave you a pair of something of mine.

RINNER: If they're nylon, I think I might be wearing them.

CINNAMON: That's nice.

RINNER: I think they might be making me do that shimmer shake.

CINNAMON: So, what I'm thinking is a cool dude might bring my panties back tonight after the show. A gal might need them. Then again, she mightn't. What think?

RINNER: You think?

CINNAMON: That all Sir Ex-ness's got to say?

RINNER: No. The thing is try not to remember too much. Bank the graces; halve the shitty bits. If it's small enough, it's the most important thing in the world... The pencil dropped in a firefight might be needed for a crossword, see?

(nods sagely but cannot seem to stop)

CINNAMON: I know, I'm going to call you my professor from now on.

RINNER: Frag-meant makes the hairy bits go over your head.

CINNAMON: Professor, professor. My hero.

RINNER: Am I?

CINNAMON: You threw a drunk out of my dressing room last night.

RINNER: I must have been drunk.

CINNAMON: Only a German trying to give Marlene Dietrich flowers.

RINNER: Was he?

CINNAMON: You often blow up like that, professor?

RINNER: Do I? Frag-meant romantic with both feet on the ground blew his top. Frag-meant star-crossed lover's head stuck in clouds. My expert witness opinion is we must all live out of suitcases, unhinged.

CINNAMON: I've always lived out of a suitcase.

RINNER: Unhinged?

CINNAMON: (sadly) I've always had to lug my spices.

43

(touches, in syncopation, his thigh, nose, nipple and his crutch)
Meet spice of life, spice of life, spice of life.
(and touches her own chest)
And pickle.

RINNER: Is my jaw dropped?

CINNAMON: Naw, your mouth is gumming up my finger.
(then, pointing upstairs)
So, all this free stuff to my people, is Professor a rich guy?

RINNER: I think I have a need to be cured of inlaws.

CINNAMON: What *I* suggest is Professor takes a teaspoonful of
nice white powder on his apricots and pistachios.

RINNER: Would that make us engaged?

CINNAMON: It sure does or Shem'll makes you dead meat.

RINNER: A toast to loaded apricots and pistachios in your
panties' sauce.

CINNAMON: *(mock toast into air)* Til we all get bored!

> *(As this has been happening, a smirking WEYDOM comes
> on to stand behind her. He is in his Interpol, spy-spoofing
> trench coat and broad-brimmed hat. CINNAMON
> obviously dislikes his over-familiarity)*

WEYDOM: You coming?

CINNAMON: Does it look like it?

> *(She pulls away to 're-emerge' into the wheelchair)*

RINNER: (nodding after her) Til we all get bored.

WEYDOM: Appropriate you're down here guarding the wheel
caps.

RINNER: Only in the quiddity of tropical sunsets are the drams dreamy and the dames underdone.
  (*has coughing fit*)
Fragmented hacker gets his own hack back.
  (*then up to WEYDOM*)
Listen, it doesn't have to be the rattle of your bare bones.

WEYDOM: Call me or Death-warmed-up, but don't call me anorexic and insult the subpoena I come to cave your sides in with.

(*He tosses the piece of paper down on RINNER'S chest*)

RINNER: Whassup?

WEYDOM: Put me down, Petey, as a friend of Ali's. Whoops, present tense. All slam the door and throw away the keys.
  (*and*)
Ali says... oops, there I go present-tense again; cut my tongue out and say wag off... they call you Frag. What's this curled up like a baby down here, 'running up the white Frag'?

RINNER: (nodding*)* Frag-meant strangers playing with each other's private parts.

WEYDOM: Jeepers, son, where do I start? Did I or did I not send you a priority letter with Rendition Travel printed all over it? So why no answer? Too much booze?

RINNER: ('booze' raises hopes*)* You here to go for a drink?
  (*WEYDOM just looks at him*)
I could show you some dry lowland rainforests *archontopheonix* mesophyll totally residual type 3a MFPVF maybe set in a minefield laid with homemade Valmara 69-type antipersonnel mines made of desert-knotted wood and lots of dead children. Very rare. Know a few drinking holes that get in the way. Rendition Travels who?

WEYDOM: You pulling my pud, Pete?

RINNER: No.

WEYDOM: So, whaddja know, Pete?

RINNER: *Nothing*!

(On-off blackout, as though he blinked. WEYDOM hasn't moved from his overbearing position.)

RINNER: What are you doing?

WEYDOM: Just climbing aboard Ali's side of the bed, son. She's so full of appetite, right? Oops, dere goes de present tense again, slice wrists, slice-slice. Anyway, like I say, I'm in, I'm slithered in. Real Interpol, me. But business first... why the deafening silence on the letters?

RINNER: No letters.

WEYDOM: Why not? Where she keeps her letters, 'kay?, and sure as shute, son, I bet you haven't even touched them. I know that coz I looked before you took your time getting home... oh, and here's Ali's key back...

RINNER: You know what Al Jolson the singer once said? He said, 'And when I get to the part where I give my present to my mammy, she looks at it a long time and says, "Diamonds... you didn't do anything wrong, did you?".

WEYDOM: So, it's still duh-duh, is it? Okay, let me explain to the all-broke. There's your Ma and Pa's travel agency in Sydney. They chose the right gal or lad as a mule, give them a Panton's uniform and free ticket and send the ticket receipt up here to Ali's safe you've got at the foot of your wardrobe there. No receipt no evidence. That's one half of the letters, then there's all the minks and things. Splash, splash, money laundering here.
    (and)
Personally I believe Pete's duh-duh. I think you're the tinkerbelle mule now, right? Hang onto that subpoena, son.

46

(rudely knocks of RINNER's head)
Knock, knock. Boarder at home up there?
(to no reply)
'Kay, I can wait. I got my toothbrush; you wanna write down your breakfast habits so I don't wake your hangover?
(afterthought)
Done a lot of things in this house, but never stayed over for breakfast.

RINNER: Shag off.

WEYDOM: My Ali can't stand the sight of me being so skinny without she bursts into tears, Pete. Pump pump, plump plump. All she wants to do was give me *flesh* by blowing some life into me, is what I think, right? It makes her cry. She's so sensitive to others she can't help herself. Heck, we both understand that now, don't we, Pete? Gee, all that present tense again.
(and)
Whoops.

RINNER: Whoops up yours.

WEYDOM: (fading with a sneer) Petey the Clown.

> *(As soon as he disappears, RINNER pitches himself at the mirror, examines himself in a maudlin way)*

RINNER: What Petey the Clown? I can't see any Petey the /Clown.

> *(He returns to sits by the phone, to continue talking into it:)*

RINNER: Little girlie, don't you go believing a word of any of that. Put it down to your poor old Dad having this febrile imagination, 'kay? Did you get that from me... you know, genetic disorders and all that?
(and)
See, all I'll say is that key to my home that dirty filthy liar claimed he returned to me was... metal.

(He simply runs out of energy.

Blackout)

8.

(Spotlight on SHEM, now 'on stage' as a shabby master of ceremony in a russet suit, under which he wears an indigenous-rights T-shirt, and what would have once been winged collar and bow tie)

SHEM: Gaydies and Gentiles, for your land-grabbing pleasure, we present from Way Up Yours, the one'n'only … or for your Latin lovers: the oon and oon-ly… or for you local Klu Klux Klannies: the goon and the goonly… the fabulous daughter of the Freedom Bus, C… C… C… Cinnamon Brown!

(Now the 'appearance' of CINNAMON again, this time heightened. She is performing her Marlene Dietrich routine on her signature bentwood chair, with black lace net stockings and legs akimbo. She is singing directly to RINNER:
Underneath the lantern by the barrack gate
Darling I remember the way you used to wait
Twas there that you whispered tenderly
That you loved me
You'd always be
My Lili of the lamplight…

As she goes through her act, SHEM is performing really basic magic tricks for the audience… with coloured handkerchiefs; with a deck of cards &ce.

He reaches over and pulls balloon out of RINNER's ear, sticks a pencil up his nose. RINNER doesn't react; he is focused so hard on CINNAMON.

What RINNER can finally do is to snap his fingers. At this,

48

CINNAMON and SHEM freeze and the music etc stops for:)

RINNER: (coarse whisper) Like I might have said, little girlie: To be honest, I wasn't ever at my best very much.

> *(CINNAMON resumes her act, this time with Holliday*
> *song:*
> *Goodbye again and if you find a love like mine,*
> *Just now and then drop a line*
> *To say you're feeling fine.*
> *And when things go wrong,*
> *Perhaps you'll see you're meant for me,*
> *So, I'll be around when she's gone.*
>
> *SHEM is continuing to get more adventurous with his side*
> *act of half-magic and half-burlesque. He is, for example,*
> *getting better juggling balls, doesn't care if they fall, and so*
> *forth; he can pull string out of unprotesting RINNER's*
> *nose.*
>
> *When CINNAMON stops singing, she doesn't leave the*
> *stage, but stands legs apart, arms akimbo beckoning*
> *customers lewdly to come up to her.*
>
> *Now that she is stationary, we can see how the strands of*
> *her net stockings dig into her fleshier thighs. She is getting*
> *fatter, less 'classy', is on the downslide as much as RINNER*
> *is.*
>
> *She laughs unattractively. She could be openly laughing at*
> *RINNER as he manages to rise and follows her beckoning.*
> *There is little respect in her voice when she addresses the*
> *audience...)*

CINNAMON: This is my Professor. If any of you haven't met him before, look in the nearest crater and say come out come out wherever you are.

> *(and she laughs with the audience, and ostensibly brushes*
> *dandruff off his hunched shoulders)*

49

RINNER: (into air) Who said 'Better luck next time'?

(*CINNAMON and SHEM fade.*

RINNER makes a dullard's way across to the mirror, peers into it, finally:)

RINNER: Dunno about next time but here's the same-same time.

(*He turns away rather sharply and with a surprising burst of energy calls:*)

RINNER: Ali, you there?

(*For a lighting-strike of a moment, ALI appears downstage, but flickers away*)

RINNER: (hope up) Ali, you there?!

(*Again, she flickers briefly into sight but then 'drops out'*)

RINNER: Ali? *Ali*!

(*but she doesn't re-appear and no amount of silent pleading will make her do so. His shoulders visibly slump.*

Blackout)

9.

(*When lighting is restored, it is partial, grainy.*

We are in some kind of dressing room, where CINNAMON removes her street clothes and merely flings them 'down'. Subserviently, RINNER retrieves them, folds or hangs them up carefully.

He kneels before her chair to take off her boots. The slightly dismissive way she allows him to do so... by keeping the 'other' foot on his shoulder, shows tellingly. When he has finished, he reaches up to roll down her panty hose, but she kicks him away.

She pointedly avoids his nearness. He sits literally at her feet, and soon nods off and starts snoring. When he does this, she kicks him awake.

SHEM's 'Cheshire-cat' head appears. He throws the appurtenances of the Disney-like clown outfit – large shoes, skull cap, trousers with braces, horse collar -- to land at RINNER's feet)

SHEM: Practise more or boom-boom, cocklehead.
  (then to his sister)
I show you this yet?

  (He shows his new trick of pulling an egg out of his mouth, then indicates RINNER)

SHEM: For cocklehead here, I'm working on a grenade instead of an egg. Hey, I'm helping with the world's surplus, ha ha, 'kay?

  (RINNER crawls off to the partly-darkened side where he can ease himself back into 'floating' with some sort of self-pitying mindlessness.

  SHEM chortles at him and fades.

  Alone with CINNAMON, RINNER looks up at her hopefully. She gives whatever he is thinking short shrift but shaking her head and turning away... it is a hurtful gesture but not done brutishly, but rather hopelessly.

  She slips out)

RINNER: Come back.

(As if to answer, MURIEL appears, 'wrapped around' WEYDOM, now back in his court-prosecutor's job.)

RINNER: Not you too, Muriel.

MURIEL: You didn't say that a couple of years ago.

RINNER: To be honest, I couldn't ever be much at my best.

WEYDOM: Is that the expert-witness's expert opinion.

RINNER: It is and it isn't. If it is, watch out for the isn't.

(They proceed to ignore his presence, resume interlocking their legs)

MURIEL: Can you explain to me how us having sex in my chambers can possibly upset your aim.

WEYDOM: Judge, my aim is intentional.

MURIEL: Well, you've just missed. Was that intentional?

WEYDOM: I headline it 'Prosecutor defrocks Judge'.

MURIEL: 'Sprays bullets everywhere'. But seriously I worry about our Rinny.

WEYDOM: It's a free world. He's just on Ice.

MURIEL: Is that a joke?

WEYDOM: It won't be when I get the Indonesians to take him and his luggage aside.

MURIEL: So, what did you say you told him?

WEYDOM: Who can tell him anything? He's gone from old boy to really old boy. That delish Madam Cinnamon opened her legs, he slipped in, and now she's got him in a vice-like grip. I tried to give the heads up.

MURIEL: What did he say?

(WEYDOM mutters unintelligibly from between her knees. She speaks directly to RINNER:)

MURIEL: Well, I'll tell you what *I* said. I said, Rinny Rinny Rinny, honestly, get up off your knees from in front of that cinnamon bun and go get happy. Ali allows. Suck hogs, not hamsters. That dandruff rain off your scurvy head has you nettlefold in a desert storm, like. And for God's sake tuck into a course of Viagra before that that Brown woman kills you. I told you you should have stayed with us grandmothers. We mightn't demand so much but we don't waste a thing.

WEYDOM: Yummy. And I said to him, 'Mate, used to be I wouldn't trust you with the Pope's daughter or the Pope's son. Now I would trust you with the Pope's daughter or the Pope's son.' Did he listen?

MURIEL: Too muffled, you think?

WEYDOM: Dope head's got his nose stuffed up with her panty hose. Want a little smoke?

MURIEL: Ah, chamber pot!

(SHEM comes back in full stage magician's get-up, pushes them aside, as, truly, the stage is now his.

He demands and gets his own spotlight. When this happens to his satisfaction, he mimes introductory flourish, shows an egg, puts it in his armpits and then proceeds, by pretty-bad sleight of hand, to pull it out of his mouth.

After self-satisfied flourish, he calls to CINNAMON)

SHEM: How's that, sis?

(gets no reply)
I said how's that?

> *(CINNAMON is caught in another spot, adjusting her panty hose guiltily. While SHEM chortles, she is defiant to RINNER)*

CINNAMON: It was only a business lunch...

> *(She walks off into the shadow. There could be someone waiting for her. There seems to be movement, whispers in the darkness.*
>
> *SHEM has more to do than worry about that, roughly gains RINNER's attention:)*

SHEM: Cocklehead, get your grubby self over here.

> *(But RINNER looks incapable of moving, so SHEM hoists the older man to his feet in centre stage, unceremoniously shoves a badly-fitting clown's latex skull cap on him)*

SHEM: Tra la la.

> *(He gets the musical fanfare he waves for. Then he balances the egg on the clown's head, covers it with a cloth. Produces a rubber hammer and makes much of aiming it at the egg.*
>
> *Unfortunately, RINNER moves, the egg rolls off and bounces – it is rubber -- to the ground. SHEM is furious for the missed trick:)*

SHEM: *You catch up or piss off!*

> *(He punches RINNER on the shoulder more contemptuously than viciously. RINNER just accepts this.*
>
> *SHEM tries again. When he gets the egg on the clown's head, he flourishes with the rubber hammer and brings it*

down. The egg smashes... it is a real one... and dribbles 'comically' down RINNER's face. He just stands there impassively

Blackout)

10.

(Lighting up on CINNAMON is about to finish her Dietrich routine...
What am I to do?
I can't help it...

While she is completing her act, RINNER stands in front of the mirror looking, unmovingly at himself. He still has the clown's latex skull cap on.

SHEM moves up behind him, picking up the clown's outfit as he goes.

RINNER just watches in the mirror as SHEM strips off his sports coat, his shirt, his trousers and then unhurriedly puts on RINNER the clown's striped shirt the baggy trousers and gaudy braces. He slips on the clown's oversized shoes as though shodding a lazy horse.

He then applies the make-up – the crosses to the eyes, the gashy lipstick.

He slips a cardboard horse collar around his neck. It is grossly outsized and hangs loosely as if in a Disney cartoon; it highlights the 'aged' scrawniness his neck seems to now have... a turtle's.

As a final coup de grace he applies the red button nose.

SHEM is having great fun... now that he can fairly

competently master the magic trick... of blowing dandruff like snow off, equally, the false cap and RINNER's head.

Finally, he claps RINNER on the shoulder, steps back to admire his handiwork.

RINNER looks at himself unemotionally)

SHEM: It looks *you*, man.
  (*then*)
Clap hands for Petey the Clown!

(A look of complicity passes between the brother and the sister.

As dullard as he now is in reaction, RINNER still sees this. He plucks off the nose. As he then tries take off the unyielding wig, SHEM is trying to put the nose back on while preventing the wig from being taken off. His playacting becomes rough to force his will upon the older man.

RINNER tries to shake his head, cannot.)

CINNAMON: Leave him alone.

SHEM: Up his. He's gotta pull his weight. Bludging.

CINNAMON: Just… leave him alone.

SHEM: All he needs is a good bomb up his arse. Hey, how about that grenade on his head, smart or what?

(Angry at them all… herself included… she tears off the wig. She hefts off the giant collar.

When she calms down enough, she speaks carefully yet firmly to RINNER)

CINNAMON: You're not the only one dog-collared around here, Professor.

SHEM: Hey, am I Manager or what?

CINNAMON: Professor, nobody asked you to… you know…
(stops to rub his back)
Breathe. Breathe.
(then)
See, nobody asked you to, shit, do all the cooking and cleaning around here. Nobody asked you to keep your eye on my all the time. Who asked you to go around wiping down all the tables, keeping the rowdies down? Dressing me, undressing me? You know? Nobody's asked you to fork out for everything. Don't keep giving him money.

(She turns on SHEM)

CINNAMON: Give him back his credit card.

(SHEM gives her the finger.)

CINNAMON: (back to RINNER) He's my family, not yours. Nobody asked you to put up with him. Nobody asked you to put up with me. I'm sorry but what gets right up my nose is not knowing if it's the fine rain of your bad dandruff or the ash from your filthy chain-smoking, you know, or...

(He has another coughing fit. She has to put her arms around him)

CINNAMON: Breathe. Okay, okay, I'll do it for both of us.
(and)
How's that?
(he nods better)
Til we all get bored. Wasn't it? Do you remember?
(he nods defeatedly)
What I'm saying is, don't let your Ali kill you. Think of it as better luck next time, or some shit like that, right?

(He is not up to answering)

CINNAMON: Say we're out to sea. It's all just bobbling along.
Just don't go bruising yourself inside. I promise I can do it for us
both now.

*(He hangs onto her in gratitude but, though gently enough,
she extracts herself.*

Blackout)

11.

*(As the lighting returns, there is intimations that it is the
bar of a Cairns hotel.*

*The music is up for the wedding celebration. A table, at
which RINNER sits, is central. He remains dressed in the
shirt and pants with braces of the clown. Though he is
trying to be reactive, he is still very dull with it.*

*The RECEPTIONIST emerges to hold RINNER by the
sleeve so he cannot escape her)*

RECEPTIONIST. Do you mind?

RINNER: Not you. Why you?

RECEPTIONIST: Excuse I, but I've only just married you in
some higher broom cupboard, that's all the thanks. I mean, you
still couldn't remember your own name.

RINNER: You're the celebrant now?

RECEPTIONIST: No need to be rude or a kick in the quoit even
if it's your honeymoon night. And do you dare talk to me about
this Cairns place, the way they treat vegetables!

58

RINNER: Vegetables what?

RECEPTIONIST: You ever been a vegetable you'd realise you don't put down roots to have some human killing machine come and rip you out of your patch. But no, you never see that on the box.

RINNER: *('what?')* Box?

RECEPTIONIST: Fermented sugar! Or goat's milk, I don't care! Show me a properly bled animal that goes the full bottle. None; so don't come the unclean over me. It's all right today, but don't do it again.

RINNER: A gain of what?

RECEPTIONIST: *(having to shout over music)* Like meat.

RINNER: Meet who?

RECEPTIONIST: Meat. Show me a country that's vegetarian that's not gone to war and still goes on about sheep's eyes in aspic. Forget the surge.

RINNER: Serge of sheep's wool?

RECEPTIONIST: It's the globs of blood. You subject them to one little bank and watch them go! The fattier they are the more they fly through space, pow! Even by sitting next to you, your brain cells are opening their phoo-phoo valves all over me, the dirty little fleshpots.

RINNER: (showing interest) You got pot?

RECEPTIONIST: Excuse I, I'll thank you for not leaning so close. I just tied your knot or something. Nice and cheeky.

(RINNER decides to wave and blink her.

MURIEL emerges on the other side of him)

RINNER: Judge, not you too!!

MURIEL: You know I can resist train wrecks, you little train wreck, you. Rinny, you are a very silly man, do you know that? How many times did I tell you to stay with us grandmothers?

(She turns away.

He leans across to an emerged CINNAMON, who says something to him, but he cannot hear for the music. She repeats it, obviously louder, but he still cannot hear her. Eventually they are able to shout enough to be heard:)

CINNAMON: My hubby the Professor… Til we all get bored?

RINNER: Til we all get bored!

(SHEM emerges to take over proceedings, calls over jute box)

SHEM: Bit of sush!
  (when he gets it)
Coupla words on this happy occasion for all youse lucky dudes'n'dudesses cos…
  (indicates RINNER of course)
he's buying. Straight up I oughta be flying up some cocklehead who reckons he can insert himself between my sister and the people, I oughta, but there's something else you oughta know...
  (pointing to MURIEL)
This's the cunt what slapped me with that 'Manslaughter' weak-as-piss verdict.

(There are the surrounding sounds of a lot of hurrahs.

MURIEL climbs to her feet in retaliation)

MURIEL: On behalf of the bridegroom-to-be, m'frag of a fragger Rinny here, who got bum-over-titted faster than I've ever seen a

60

bum going over a tit and I ought to know, I would like to insert into these proceedings...
(pointing back to SHEM)
He's the cunt what made me do it!

> *(SHEM acknowledges the equality of her response and, still in charge, moves around behind RINNER)*

SHEM: (to RINNER) On your feet, Witless!

> *(The others join in a chorus of 'On your feet, Witless', until RINNER finally does.*
>
> *From there, SHEM shows his new magic trick of producing eggs from RINNER's one ear, then the other. Then he turns to CINNAMON, produces a bride's bouquet and also eggs. Then urges her on to be a broody hen. She obliges willingly:)*

CINNAMON: Bok bok bok...

> *(Milking this gag, SHEM nudges RINNER to mimic a rooster.*
>
> *RINNER starts off reluctantly, timing his rooster call with her hen's bokking, until – slowly but rising to the unstoppable -- he releases his grief about ALI at last:)*

RINNER: Cockle-doodle-do. Cockle-doodle-do. Cockle-doodle-do!
(until he rings out)
COCKLE-DOODLE-DO! COCKLE-DOODLE-DO!

(End Act 2)

61

Act 3
12.

(RINNER is in half light in his apartment and alone on stage)

RINNER: (into air) That's better! Better out than in, my old Mum used to say. Better throw up than toss it in, she used to say. That's what your Granny was like, little girlie

(Now general, but the usual pale, lighting up on the bare apartment where RINNER is alone with the phone.

He remains in his clown's clothes although still confined to the striped shirt and trouser-with-braces.

He is lying down beside the phone, ostensibly listening to it… nodding and grunting conversationally as it goes.

When it is apparently polite enough to do so, he gets up lethargically and goes over to the mirror. Nothing he sees is any better)

RINNER: Mirror, mirror…

(stops to return to lie down next the phone, carries on listening, before:)

RINNER: By the way, ickle Deesie of mine, that 'Mirror, Mirror' had nothing to do with the one about the guy talking to a mirror. Just so you know; I wouldn't want you to think your old Dad was trying to string you along. My little girl. My little girlie.

(He stands in a conscious attempt to start all over again)

RINNER: Little girlie, I think I've done this before but I don't want to take the chance of missing you, so what the hell… Next week's too far away!

*(As he did in the early part of Act 1, he extracts an airmail
letter from his pocket, reads a phone number and goes back
and dials STD... again it is more of a conversation with the
audience rather than someone in Amsterdam:)*

RINNER: Hello! Is that...
   (gets cut off, redials irritably)
Kindly don't come that again. Dee Rinner, please. *Dee Rinner.*
Hey, look, you speak English? No, I'm speaking English! No, I
don't speak Dutch. Is there...
   (has to listen again)
No, I still don't speak Syrian. Sorry, no Sudanese Arabic either.
Look, Dee Rinner there? Who? No, shissake, I'm not speaking
Indonesian. It's Australian. No, what's the use of me trying to take
language lesson; didn't I say I was Australian? Kindly pull the
wool out.
   (lying like a dog)
Me? You serious? Well, I might be a dad, but sprightly like you
wouldn't guess. Thick black on top, not a jungle clearing in sight.
Tall, some say debonair but I usually demur. I'm the type for
which it's a shame video phones haven't come in too much yet,
say so m'self. Married, me? No, no; only a few bits hanging off
me. So, now that you have me down to a T, d'think my
daughter's coming to the phone? Sure, I'll hang on. Why not it's
been nineteen years, so what's a minute or two between friends?
Sure, you and me remain friends. Would we be having moonlight
dinners if we weren't, ha ha?

   *(He holds his head in his hands to control his frustration,
   then turns back to the mobile to try again)*

RINNER: Whazzat? Sure you'd fit in in Australia. Yes, you'd
be allowed to divorce me if you wanted to. No, Australia's farther
away from Austria than Rio. What do you mean it's the dogs?
No, I've got nothing to do with them letting the dogs roam all
around the Amsterdam airport shitting on the floor while the
Dutch authorities are giving you a hard time. I don't... I don't...

   *(But gives it trying to get a word in edgeways. He lies back
   on the floor by the phone... obviously now a familiar place*

for him)

RINNER: (*into air*) Still there, little girlie? Of course you're still there. Anyway, I can tell you in all honesty, there was no way I could ever say to your mother that no male in the Rinner side has ever survived to see in the next pregnancy. I mean, lying there avoiding the prospect of sex with Ali thinking about how wonderful our sex with her was. It was all very difficult. I'm only human, you know.

(has to listen)

What? Yeah, I thought I might have already told you all that. The old synapses snapping, eh, ha ha? So, did I tell you about 'Better luck next time' and 'Til we all get bored'? No? Don't ask me why, I just can't get them out of my head, that's all. Just never say Dodo, your granny used to say.

(and)

Ssh. I wrote something down for you. Ssh. It's…

(rumples through his pocket to find inside of cigarette packet)

'Snatches now, blurred, olden, nehe? Only our memories are probably staying bobbing substantial, zephyrs of past crafts, in this sea, this sea.'

(throws packet away)

Ssh. Needs a bit of work, admittedly. Sush.

> *(Absent-minded all of a sudden, he goes to mirror again. Looks at same-old, same-old)*

RINNER: (chuckles) Moonlight dinners… I hate having to talk sickly mush when I trying to chew.

(Blackout)

13.

(Lingeringly, lighting up on the foyer and reception area of the hotel. Even the 'faded' light of the staging gives the heyday of the place as being a very long time ago. The time is the present though.

The receptionist, MAIYAH, and the general hand, HUKKA, are at the desk. She is a small dark shrewish Eurasian woman of Batavian-Chinese immigrant stock; he a main-chancer Maori – both dubiously without proper papers to be working in the country.

RINNER is leaning across the reception desk. He has just arrived.

When the scene opens, the three of them are staring into each other's eyes from the distance of only a few millimetres.

Finally, and without moving a millimetre, RINNER:)

RINNER: I'll try to explain again. Speaka da…?

(MAIYAH and HUKKA gesture 'Hold it!'. They put on pollution face masks, then resume their open-eyes eyeballing of RINNER while he speaks right into their faces from extreme close-up…)

RINNER: See, I've come around the world to see my daughter. I'm hot. I'm tired. I've just been on a twenty-hour flight with a monstrous Japanese kid still in diapers but twenty kilos overweight to be a Sumo wrestler constantly dropping that great Sumo-wrestler's head of his onto my lap like I was Pearl Harbour and the last dying throes of USS *Missouri*. And all the time his fucking mother was having a lovely time, out to the world in the seat on the other side of him until they took her away for an overdose xray when we landed. I mean, this kid was so gigantic they had to bring equipment up to unload him off the plane. And I'm telling you, that head could have belonged to the Prime Minister of Australia. I couldn't eat, drink, shift my bum. I had to ask for a straw so I could reach my whiskey. They said the only thing they had long enough was the fire hose. For twenty hours, all I could do was count my cramps. Now for one small room, I beg you. Even a broom cupboard would do.
    (*then*)

65

So?

> (MAIYAH and HUKKA just stare back ungivingly. By way
> of answer, they produce signs that look like street-protest
> placards. Hers reads: NO ROOM. His reads: MARLENE
> DIETRICH STAYED HERE.

> There is another eye-to-eye stasis, such that RINNER
> doesn't notice his daughter entering from the street. She is
> twenty-one and tall beneath her thick layers of what look
> like cast-off gypsy clothing and her unruly and over-
> henna'd hair. She would not be the neatest person ever to
> meet a father after nineteen years. Casually she comes up
> and pokes him roughly on the shoulder.

> When he turns around he is in shock, looks quite capable of
> taking flight)

RINNER: Dee?

> (He goes to move to her, gets entangled up with his
> briefcase and literally falls flat on his face at her feet.

> He stays there, groans in pain with his ankle. She doesn't
> bend to help, only giggles and then reveals a shocking
> idiomatic Scottish accent)

DEE: Dar, what are ye doin' down under, ha ha?

RINNER: Oh, God, your mother's turned you into a Scottish git.

DEE: Is wha' they say aboot Australyen men true then?

RINNER: What, what?

DEE: Tha' when they see a skirt they tryta measure their length,
ha ha?

RINNER: Wait, wait. Get my breath.
> (then, even though he still can't get up)

66

Old grand final injury. The Four'n'Twenty queue.
    (*and attempts*)
Dee! My little girlie!

DEE: Dunno about tha', goin' so far, like.

RINNER: (waving futilely) See, that.

DEE: Wha'?

RINNER: That, that. Talk like that. I'm here. Daddy's come.

DEE: Aye. Well, for a start, a' wouldna be boastin' aboot tha' a'll.

RINNER: (tries desperate joke) You tell your mother that the first thing I did after nineteen years was throw myself at your feet.

DEE: (looking at own feet) Forgot t'paint tha' toenails this mornin'.

RINNER: Do you think you could help me up?

DEE: (giggle) You're got a bit o' a billiard ball on top.

RINNER: I'm not the only father with a comb-over! If you can't give me a kiss, give me a hand?

DEE: Got a bit o' a cold sore, Dar. Ye wouldna like tha'.

RINNER: (anguish) It doesn't have to be a kiss on the lips!

DEE: Well, m'top lip's reactin' to th'Clearosil. Might be a bit oozy.

RINNER: Gimme the back of your hand then!

DEE: But y'doant know where any of the others are, do ye?

RINNER: What others?

67

DEE: Cold sores. Maybe tomorrow. Weather forecast's good then.

RINNER: Oh, Christ. I think I've done my ankle.

DEE: Ma said tha' only thing ye ever got close to help y'self oop, like, wa' t'jump oop'n'down in front a th'fridge lookin' for food.

RINNER: That's a downright lie told in the Family Court!

DEE: Wha' I didna believe was they had fridges back tha' far, like.
   (*then*)
Well, runnin' late, Dar. Maybe I'll see ye later.

RINNER: *(*desperate*)* Help me up. I'll show you I'm not always writhing!

DEE: Naw, Dar, I've got the second floor windows. After tha', I've got to finish a whole bottle of tha' gin, ain't I?

RINNER: What?

DEE: Before the bath water gets cold, aye. It comes with a right hot bath thrown in.

RINNER: What?

DEE: Best thing is they throw is a brown paper bag if ye'd like a souvenir, like.
   (*swings around to the others*)
Y'hear this one, Maiyah? 'Ladies and gentlemen, this is your Captain speakin'. If ye look out left ye ken see Amsterdam. If ye look out right ye kin see smoke from tha engines. If you look straight down ye'll see a lifeboat floatin' in tha water. It is from there tha' your Captain is speakin''.

RINNER: I told you that over the phone yesterday! Dee, don't go! Look down; it is from there your father is speaking!

68

DEE: Dar, doctor warned not to touch anyone 'til tha tincture o' iodine wears orf. Well, seeya soon…

RINNER: At least tell me you miss me!

DEE: Tha's wha' my mates used t'say. 'Don't ye miss your Dar afta all these year?' I'd say, 'Not if I take careful aim, like'.

RINNER: Don't say that! Why'd you say that?
 (*she is gone*)
Why'd she say that?

   (*Blackout*)

14.

(*Lighting comes back on in the hotel foyer. It is the same as before… RINNER, MAIYAH and HUKKA are locked in a silent danse macabre with the eyes from only a few millimetres away. Again, RINNER has obviously only just arrived.*

Over-extended pause. When it seems nobody is ever going to give way, RINNER shouts:)

RINNER: NO, NO! TRY AGAIN!

(*Again, MAIYAH and HUKKA quickly don pollution face masks to avoid getting any germs from him, since he speaks from being right up into their faces*)

RINNER: You should be thankful I'm not pressing my present genetic material on either of you. See, nineteen years ago, I'm sure we would have lived troppo if my little girlie had chosen me. No, no, not because they don't enforce restriction orders much up the Far North. I'm talking about those corals. No, I'm not. I don't know what's gotten into me. Yes, I do. It's not having a room.

See, up there, there's a hotel called the Cairns Colonial Coitus…
something like that… and it had this pet bandicoot running around
its garden at nights. With all those inner thighs open under the
tables, lucky little perv, says I; hope it's got binocular vision.
Anyway, one night some American tourist thinks it's a dirty great
rat and beats the living bells out of it. Rare as hen's teeth, those
tropical bandicoots. This endangered one got endangered all right.
So the hotel gets anotheree and this time puts up a sign saying,
'NO BASHING OUR DIRTY GREAT RAT.' What I'm trying to
say is: the signs might be wrong but don't beat me, I'm the only
endangered species you've got.

> *(Finished, they resume the silent eyeballing for a further
> moment, until, this time, HUKKA holds up the NO ROOM
> sign and MAIYAH holds up the MARLENE DIETRICH
> STAYED HERE sign.*
>
> *Again, too, this is the time DEE comes in from the street
> without being seen by her father. She is breathless. She
> stops short when it is obvious this is her father, but this time
> she waits respectfully in the open, motions to MAIYAH not
> to tell him yet.*
>
> *She is dressed now noticeably differently – much better
> groomed and fashionably modern -- modish, classy,
> carefully turned out -- and when she speaks it is only with a
> faint and charming Scottish lilt.*
>
> *MAIYAH taps RINNER on the shoulder, points out what's
> behind him. He turns. There is the same awkward,
> wonderful moment of seeing each other for the first time in
> nineteen years)*

DEE: Dad?

> *(This time he moves to her joyously and gets there without
> tripping, even though he still stumbles over briefcase. They
> embrace nervously, then fiercely. They hold it there.
> Finally,)*

DEE: Oh, it's lovely to see you.

RINNER: I thought I'd lost you again before I found you again.

DEE: I just couldn't see you anywhere at the airport.

RINNER: Would you have recognised me anyway?

DEE: *(laughing)* No.

RINNER: I should have worn a sign, 'Whoever's holding the short straw, here's your dirty great tropical bandicoot'.

DEE: Mum said you'd trot out the humour.

RINNER: What else she say?

DEE: Not to bother to laugh because it wouldn't be funny, ha ha.

(They hug again. All couldn't be going better)

RINNER: I can't believe how beautiful you've grown.

DEE: I waited. I waited until there was one bag going around the roundabout. Mum said that would be yours.

RINNER: Shit, I've left it behind!

DEE: Mum said that's why it'd be yours.

RINNER: She's so smart, did she tell you it's the one with all your presents in it?

DEE: Oh.

RINNER: I'm joking. I didn't bring any.
  (quickly)
I know, she said that too. Great woman, that mother of yours. Discerning chooser of men.

71

DEE: *(tearfully)* I wanted to cry when nobody came for that last bag.

RINNER: I booked us into adjoining rooms.

DEE: No, Dar, I'm just down the corridor with the other staff.

RINNER: Hey, it might be a long corridor.

DEE: The bus service is good.

RINNER: And you've got young legs.

DEE: And I've got young legs, yes.

> *(They can now enjoy and pause. In this, HUKKA, with exaggerated professionalism, picks up his briefcase)*

HUKKA: This way, sir.

> *(He goes to follow HUKKA out, stops)*

RINNER: It doesn't seem real, does it? I bet your mother said I'd say that too.

DEE: (nodding) She said you wouldn't know what's real and what's not, ha ha.

RINNER: She's a real joker that mother of yours.

DEE: Dar, she said to tell you she never found it a joke.

> *(He turns to follow HUKKA again, not knowing the latter has returned impatiently and has put his briefcase back on the floor.*
>
> *RINNER gets tangled up in it again and crashes down. There is a cry of pain.*
>
> *Lighting transfer to:)*

15.

(RINNER in spotlight back on phone in his apartment. He seems to sink into a delirium as he goes with:)

RINNER: Now that didn't hurt, did it? Yes, it bloody did. Little girlie, just put it down to us falling into each other's arms, kiss, kiss, watch out the earth's moving. In my heyday... HEY, GET THE TROUGH OUT; I'VE GOT THE SNOUT!... no, listen, in my heyday with the Children's Fund, I always thought I'll get through what I had to lay my eyes on by reckoning I could live on it for the rest of my working days, y'know? What I didn't take on board is that when you leave they give you an ashes urn to put your burn-out in. Little girlie, I have to tell you I saw the bruise-ups and the beat-ups the eaten-ups, the diseased-up, yet all that time I grieved for you. I could pick most of little'uns up in the palm of my hand, you know? How many holding palms can a man have, you ask? Many, oh many! So, after I did my work-a-days but every story kept coming out like 'All the Fund's li'l chil'run no fun at all'. Something like that. I lashed out with the pills with the salt and held their arms for the jabs. I swabbed the gunk from their little eyes with the magic cottons. But I grieved for you. I still think of most of them waving their little arms and legs like they were out of their depth and signalling for help. What can I do? What I mean, do you know? I was only trying to make an honest living. But there are bandages and their ulcers. There are their little bums and any old, any old, cloth, you know?, to wipe the droppingdripping shittiness off of them. Too many, that's the thing. Too many no I'm not your Mummy and no I'm not your Daddy and getting the look. But all the time I was only grieving for you. I think there's a full stop there.

(simply stops. Lighting transfer to:)

16.

(The hotel foyer where RINNER is sitting at the bar, left. He has his ankle in plaster.

Seated along from him is the WOMAN IN VEIL who sits with her back to him evidently looking out of the window. While RINNER often sneaks a look at her, she doesn't return it... only that, increasingly often, she will snigger at something he says or is said about him.

DEE is coming to him. She is now back to her slovenly look, with her caricature accent. She is almost halfway through some dirty cleaning chore and hasn't bothered to clean up)

DEE: How ye feelin' t'day, old cock?

RINNER: (sarcastically*)* You got lost trying to visit me in hospital?

DEE: Got this itch, Dar. They wouldna let me in. What ye drinkin'?
   (helps herself to his drink)
Busy, busy. I like ta finish before dark, y'ken? A' nights I like a bit a the Dutch stuff, when I'm nae at the hot tubs n' gin. Dutchies're chuffy a' their finger pokes in dykes n' wha'nots, ha ha. Doant think I'm not thinkin' of you, but.
   (then)
Ha' ye always been such a stumblebum, Dar?

RINNER: (at WOMAN IN VEIL's back) Nineteen years. My own daughter can't even get around to visit her father in hospital.

DEE: Sookie. It's only a broken ankle or sumthin', like.

RINNER: It's connected by pain to the rest of my body!

DEE: Say, Dar, y'still like a bit o' the old guzzle too much?

74

RINNER: (hot retort) Does your mother still have warts on where she gets fingered?

DEE: She ha' them cut oot, ye should know tha'. Ye paid for it.

RINNER: I couldn've done it with a Swiss army knife for free.

DEE: An' she had her bum tightened while she were a' it. Then extra for tha' putty work remodellin', like. Then a month in tha' Swiss clinic getting tha nerve ends massaged back. Subcutaneous, tha's it. N' the subcutaneous injections to get her bum the right overall tan. N' my bum while she were at it an' you were payin'. Wanna see?

RINNER: God forbid.

DEE: Tha's nuffin' on your credit card compared to her nose job an' fixin' her teeth an' straighten that eye o' hers. N' the wrinkles n' tha cellulite stuff n' the tummy job. Then tha' whole lot o' teeth ha' to be done again. Nice o' you, Dar. Mum says thank ye if I get cornered, like.

RINNER: Tell her it's high time she had a better profile of our time together than my American Express card.

DEE: I told her wha' ye doant ken didna hurt ye.

RINNER: Look, Dee, you think you can speak English?

DEE: Wha'?, after tha Scottish referendum? Oh, an' the bags under her eyes, like, an' the chin n' tha hips liposuctions n' all. She looks a million now with tha breast enhancement an' the nipples sensitized. Och, ye oughta gleep tha' fellahs crowdin' around her in tha' bikini. Nice. She digs Nice for her hols these days.

RINNER: Don't tell me... on me.

DEE: She said you'd twig. Wha' she puts it like is she went into th'marriage with ye on a once-only daily proposition an' came out as a multiple entry ona monthly credit-card statement. Ha, ha.

RINNER: Ha, ha.

DEE: Well, Dar, ha' to get back a' work.

RINNER: Dee, stay and talk! Give me some time!

DEE: Actually, Dar, it was toss oop if I should meet ye at all.

RINNER: Don't say that!

DEE: (cunningly) I thought a silicon job like Mum's an' see if they kin make m'eyes a wee wider, like, an' a touch a body contourin' an' pad a few cheeks here'n'there… wanna nother feel?

RINNER: Charge it all to me, just stay!

DEE: She told me ta say that too an' then… *run like th'bejesuses!*

> *(With crazy humour, she takes off, leaving him devastated.*
> *He adds defensively to WOMAN IN VEIL's back)*

RINNER: That was my daughter. I thought we could fill in the time around the art galleries, Rembrandt land, Van Gogh, the opera, a bit of experimental theatre and jazz in Melkwig, but mainly strolling the canals, drinking coffee, chin wagging, boulevarding with the best. Let her savour the feeling of truly belonging.
  (*to a snigger from the woman*)
Pardon me, Madam, but you wouldn't read about what ex's can say about you, would you? I mean, this is a woman who used to need a royal corgi implant to attract a flea-bitten street dog.
  (*maudlin*)
I wanted my little girlie to be a doctor, an opera singer, a physicist, not some Billie Holliday even if they call her Lady Day.

> *(The WOMAN IN VEIL gets up and leaves)*

76

RINNER: (after her) All I got was an expert in gin bath tubs.

(He stares after her. He is rewarded when DEE reappears, reverted to her neater, less caricatured self. He starts up as though she had never left)

RINNER: You know, where we lived, by the time you were eight you'd been around the world twice?

DEE: I remember a dog. Was there a dog?

RINNER: You remember Hephaestus? A great Dane. He leant on you like a drunk.

DEE: Some pig?

RINNER: Yes! Boris! We were on the island of Fomentara off Spain. We had the Roman salt mine and its jetty to ourselves. We had this well for water down past Boris's sty. We fattened him up on our scraps. He'd stand up and put his front legs over the sty gate and start chewing madly away at the rock wall there, food-food. More than half starved. Poor old Boris. One morning when I was trying to get a last sleep-in, there was Boris right outside the door squealing... well, like a pig. I jumped out of bed, threw open the door, grabbed old Boris and threw him onto the cart there. When I got back to bed I thought, oh Jesus what have I done?

DEE: Not to market?

RINNER: (nodding) You see how it goes? You think you're doing some good then one day along comes a blood rush to the head and you go and chuck it. That old lady from the farm cackled at me every time she saw me after that. Boris.

DEE: *(now nodding)* What Mum called the Boris Effect.

RINNER: You're kidding.

DEE: She shrugs and says, 'The Boris Effect'. Under her breath like.

RINNER: When?

DEE: I don't know. Odd times. When she feels let down. No, it was more than that. Maybe something like betrayed, I think.

RINNER: How she going?

DEE: Getting engaged. But don't ask me. I haven't met him.

RINNER: You haven't met your future step-father?

DEE: Not much interested, Dar.

RINNER: (cheeringly) We on for tonight?

DEE: I'm getting dolled up an' I'm so hungry I'm eating an oily baby sideways, aye.

> *(She kisses his cheek and leaves.*
>
> *Still ignoring him, the re-emerged WOMAN IN VEIL rings for a drink. When HUKKA comes, she merely holds up her empty crème de menthe glass for refill. Signs the chit without turning properly around.*
>
> *RINNER takes the opportunity of pushing his own glass forward for renewal. It is deliberately ignored by HUKKA who simply walks back down the corridor. MAIYAH intervenes:)*

MAIYAH: No mind him. We invite him to our wedding.

RINNER: I'm forgetting my wedding now?

MAIYAH: You promise o'er phone. Big fat liar. Wha' a pig!

> *(Blackout)*

17.

(RINNER on floor by the phone in is apartment. As he speaks ALI comes under a spot)

RINNER: How are you, Ali, my Ali?

ALI: I still remember you.

RINNER: I've been overseas all the time, my Ali. I might still be.'

ALI: And before that?

RINNER: I know, I know. Moving. The thing is, my Ali, I've got this lump thing I'm watchfully waiting on.

ALI: Oh.

RINNER: I love you, see, that's the thing. Forgive me if I've become a bit sweaty.

ALI: How bad's that lump thing?

RINNER: A little less wobbly for talking to you, Ali. Ali?

ALI: Yes.

RINNER: 'See, I've bought this apartment in Sydney but it's on the back of the little'uns all over Africa and other places, you know?

ALI: I know.

RINNER: And, well, it's bad money, Ali. I think I'm deep down corrupt, Ali. What do you reckon? Do you think you might get past that snake and come back to me?

ALI: What's that Sydders apartment like?

RINNER: Ferny. But I keep locking my keys in, see.

ALI: I like the fur stoles in Sydney.

RINNER: Come take a look at it, Ali.

ALI: As long as no pegging out before I get there.

RINNER: I will watchfully wait here, Ali, my Ali.

(He gently turns away as though 'allowing' her to go. When she has faded, he moves over to the mirror, and:)

RINNER: Don't tell your mother we mentioned the word gin, that's all. *She* might have weak kidneys but she was always onto me. I mean, those empties she found in the shed were four-months' supply. She tried to make out it was three months. How insulting can you get?! I'm a newspaper man. Back then I was *supposed* to breath whisky fumes on my baby. I take a sip of vino at the dinner table and she's covering up your little eyes. She did. She said it wasn't the wine but because it was such cheap plonk. I said whoa up, the truth like that in front of the baby hurts more than any whisky breath. You know what I think, little girlie? You think I'm bad mouthing your mother. Never! How could I when she spent all the housekeeping on Listerine? All I'm saying I could have been teaching you to say Daddah with a clap-hands-paddy-whack but I get home from work one night and I find she's taught you to say it with one of her bits-of-yawns, baby-version. You've got this bib on inscribed with "I don't drink'. And I don't know if you know that time they sent me out to Rwanda. Nineteen ninety four, April, near your other birthday. Someone shouted quick get out to Musha Church. So we pile into a jeep and off we go. It was pretty much that burnt-out shell on TV by the time we got there. Pretty well all-new – I joke -- Tutsi charred corpses still there, though. I think we gave up counting after a thousand. I didn't. Give up. I counted around two hundred children alone on the top of the piles, as though they were trying to pass them to the top of the piles for when God would just have to take pity on them and unlocked those God-horror of doors. What is it about God and keys? What will they unlock when you want them to? So, anyway, I went outside and threw up. A little hand took mine. I looked down. It was a little girl without a face. I think she didn't have a face. I know she didn't have a face. I'm positive she didn't have a... you know...

> *(He remains defeated, motionless for enough time to allow MAIYAH – she stays within her spotlight – to dance traditional Javanese grotesquely. She does so with gongs and gamelans and eventually comes near enough to his spotlight to:)*

MAIYAH: Now we alone.

RINNER: No, thanks.

MAIYAH: You rejected. I marree rejects all time. Do you self favour. I come from royal line of Java. Big time princess.

RINNER: You're a Javanese princess now?

MAIYAH: Got ancestors in box seat. You come Maiyah's room tonight on promise you take Rio an' I show right royal box.

RINNER: If I can fit a Dutch clog up my nose, I'll think about it.

MAIYAH: Put up dukes. You no talk to a Javanese princess like tha'.

RINNER: No, really, you find me that clog and I will. No, see, what you're getting mixed up with is you think you're Mata Hari. It's not Mata Hari, it's Marlene Dietrich who stayed here.

MAIYAH: (sulkily) How I remember all the name an' face pass through here?

> *(He turns from her so that she can next fade off. He gets back into phone)*

81

RINNER: That woman is an inspirational to us all!

(When he looks up again, DEE has appeared. She is the untidy, disrespectful one)

DEE: Dar, I've bin thinkin', like. It's ba' enough inside here, like, but oot in tha' wide world wid ye so everyone ken see... och, well, tha's a wee bit harsh, Dar.

RINNER: Did I miss something?

DEE: Tha' Aussie accent. Any chance ye cud change it a wee bit?

RINNER: What Aussie accent? What about that bagpipe squeaking out of your nose of yours?

(She disappears. He looks around, but up in the air, and it is to the phone that he addresses:)

RINNER: Where'd you go?

(HUKKA and MAIYAH appear as if this was a cue)

HUKKA: Hey, bub, which part of Aussie you from?

RINNER: From the past part.

HUKKA: That past Brisbane?

RINNER: No, down south. South past Austria. Maiyah knows that.

MAIYAH: I no speak you. Where my engagement ring?

RINNER: (still to HUKKA) Way past when.

HUKKA: That past Sydney?

RINNER: Even down past there.

HUKKA: Nothing's down past there.

RINNER: Yes, there is. There's Auckland.

HUKKA: Yeah? You past fifty?

RINNER: A fly past.

HUKKA: Past sixty?

RINNER: (*nodding*) Given what's just past.

HUKKA: Nar, nothing's past sixty or you'd be way past
Tasmania.

RINNER: I guess I would.

HUKKA: Well past it.

RINNER: Oh, I am, I am.
  (*aloud*)
Has anyone told my daughter I've arrived?

MAIYAH: She go to airport.

RINNER: Oh God, I knew I'd missed her.

MAIYAH: (snigger as well) He believe anything!

   (*MAIYAH and HUKKA fade*)

RINNER: Where're you gone? Where's she gone?

   (*as instantly as possible, the mocking, cud-chewing DEE is
   back*)

DEE: Och, married men are ye on about now

83

RINNER: What?

DEE: Ye show me a married man gettin' caught red-handed, like, because his troosers are all twisted n' he can't get his other leg through an' you're sittin' up tryin' t'look all innocent like.

RINNER: What?

DEE: Mind ye, I'm all right with the children with spouts in Africa, Ethiopia an' all tha'. It's past tha' age of ten where I draws tha' line, like.

RINNER: *What*?!
  (*then, as though it matters*)
No wonder my side of your family doesn't have any grandfathers. You want to know why?

DEE: Sure, Dar. Jus' let me get shot o' this bit of chewie first.

  (and moves off, cudding. He has to heighten his outrage after her)

RINNER: I'll tell 'ye' why! Her grandfather left my mother a few years after I was born and we don't talk about it. Her great grandfather left my grandmother a few years after my father was born. We don't talk about that. Her great great wouldabeen grandfather left his wife a few years after my great grandfather was born and we don't talk about that either. In 1854, her great great great somethingorother grandfather jumped ship at Adelaide and left his wife a few years after my daughter's great great somethingorother grandfather was born. He never spoke about it but I know we're really from Adelaide not New Zealand where the ship was headed. All I know is smartarses don't have grandfathers tucked away somewhere. So put that in the crack in your pipe and smoke it!

  (Blackout)

18.

(During the interim, and gradually, CINNAMON's singing Billie Holliday on stage grows louder:
All of me
Why not take all of me
Can't you see I'm not good without you
Take my lips; I want to lose them
Take my arms, I'll never use them

This then fades.

Then, AS ACTED OUT BEFORE:

SHEM reappears, now fully dressed in his magi magician's get-up. He mimes introductory flourish, shows an egg, puts it in his armpits and then proceeds, by pretty-bad sleight of hand, to pull it out of his mouth. After self-satisfied flourish, he calls to CINNAMON)

SHEM: How's that?
 (gets no reply)
I said how's that?

> *(CINNAMON is caught in another spot in street clothes, adjusting her pantyhose guiltily)*

CINNAMON: I said it was just a business lunch...

> *(She walks off into the shadow. There could be someone waiting for her. There seems to be movement, whispers in the darkness.*
>
> *This has no importance to SHEM)*

SHEM: Cocklehead, get your X-marks-the-spot over here.

> *(From the mirror, RINNER obediently goes over to him. SHEM unceremoniously shoves on the clown's red nose and Disney horse collar.*

*He gets the musical fanfare he wants. He balances the egg
on the clown's head, covers it with a cloth. Produces a
rubber hammer and makes much of aiming it at the egg. But
RINNER moves, and the egg rolls off and bounces – it is
rubber -- to the ground)*

SHEM: *(furious) You catch up or piss off!*

*(He punches RINNER on the shoulder more
contemptuously than viciously. RINNER just accepts this.*

*SHEM tries again. When he gets the egg on the clown's
head, he flourishes with the rubber hammer and brings it
down. The egg smashes... it is a real one... and dribbles
'comically' down RINNER's face. He just stands there
taking it.)*

RINNER: (dully) We've done all this.

19.

(Lighting back up on RINNER at the mirror)

RINNER: Little girlie, where aren't we in watch of the tropical
drum thrum of our own inner things?
    (*plus*)
Better luck next time.

(Muriel appears behind him)

MURIEL: Rinny, you little buggerlugs, stop giving yourself
pimples over there. Go home; sit where Ali was sitting when…
well, never mind that. What've you and your inlaws been up to,
anyway? Honestly, Rinny, them into bigtime drugs, sheeee. Suck
hogs, not hamsters. And for God's sake get in a course of rhino
horns before that Cinnamon sucks the marrow right out of you. I

told you you should have stayed with us grandmothers. We know how to keep the oozing dripping like a tap.

(She fades after he just stares at her for a long moment.

'Falling in Love Again' returns in sound and finished.

CINNAMON, in her Marlene Dietrich costume, steps 'down' and moves to WEYDOM now shown sitting – obviously at a table watching the show and, by shadow effects, with a group of hooting male friends. CINNAMON barely glances RINNER's way, but goes straight towards WEYDOM's table to pass the interval.

With mock heroics, WEYDOM takes off his jacket and covers her shoulders. He takes her hand and kisses the back of it, all the time looking over at RINNER and smirking.

Blackout)

20.

(RINNER in spotlight. He now has on the full Petey the Clown regalia – the Disney horse collar, the plaffy shoes, the red button nose etc)

RINNER: Once you were like a koala in my arms. I took my little koala onto the great ancient steps of the theatre of Zea in Piraeus. I carried her onto the ancient stage of the Alexandrian amphitheatre in Alexandria. I waltzed her onto the apron of the great old Philippopolis amphitheatre in Plodiv in Bulgaria. I said to her, 'This is where your old Dad truly belongs'. Your mother said from the Gods, 'Thank God that took only 2000 years to figure out'.

(When there is a 'nightspot' drum roll, he flops down to

floor.

SHEM comes on stage, dressed, confidently now, in his magician's outfit. Flourishes with egg in one hand, a grenade in the other)

SHEM: Yo, sinners and sunburners... what's it gonna be, egg or grenade?

(He milks the inevitable call for the grenade, comes over and rudely hoists RINNER to his feet, hauls him stage side, then goes through the routine of placing it on Petey the Clown's head, using the rubber hammer to stand well back and, when timing is right, brings the hammer down on the grenade.

It is an egg in reality. Again the humiliation is there as the egg dribbles down RINNER'S face. But the applause is muted this time. RINNER has sympathy from the audience. Some small boos.

SHEM gives them the middle-finger and leaves.

RINNER shuffles back to where he was, flops down again.

CINNAMON extracts herself from WEYDOM, comes over, cups RINNER's face)

CINNAMON: Oh. Oh.

RINNER: *(*expressionless*)* Oh.

CINNAMON: Why the sad face, Professor?

RINNER: Hello.

CINNAMON *(*of his body odour*)* Phew.
  (and)
They were only business lunches.

RINNER: Runcible.

CINNAMON: Runcible, huh?

RINNER: Runcible. Funcible no.

CINNAMON: What's that mean?

RINNER: Good, do god dogod the gob. No sweat.

CINNAMON: So, how do I look?

RINNER: Beautiful, Cinnamon of that name. Remember when you answered once in bed: Til we all get bored?

CINNAMON: It didn't mean anything

RINNER: Frag-meant all gets a shard.

> (He laughs in an ugly way at this. It comes over as actually laughing in her face. She reels from it as though it was a slap in the face... and keeps moving backward until she is out of sight.
>
> Blackout.)

21.

(RINNER hasn't bothered to take off the full Petey the Clown outfit. But he is back in the centre of his apartment with his phone and:)

RINNER: Talking about this mirror, did I ever tell you the one about the guy who walked up to this mirror and said, 'Mirror, Mirror, on the wall, who is the fairest of them all?' and the mirror says...
   (starts again)

RINNER: Little girlie, little Dee, see, the Fund sent me back there to Rwanda that time, you ever remember? The Hutus… or maybe from the Tutsis… hard to tell them it didn't matter. Thousands of them crossing back over the border who could even think about asking them how're you going to survive the floods? The biggest locust plague in a century? The dysentery, the diarrhea, watching the cholera take hold of all my kids… There was this vast glue pot of mud left after the landslide outside the camp. I couldn't pull them all out; how could I? I had a little hand and I pulled and she came out and I think the little thing's mouth was grinning at me. See, the thing is… there were these small crabs all over her face. They had taken her features. She didn't have a face left either. Everywhere I seem to go there were no faces and a lot of these rotten little crabs…

   (*then*)

You hear the one about the crippled crab? It travelled from Melbourne to Sydney on a crutch.

   (*and*)

So I went back to the New York headquarters and I shouted at them: 'Do you fuckers have any idea there's a little girl out there with no face, two little girls out there with no face, three little girls out there with no face… dozens of them… hundreds of them, whole gangs of hundreds of thousands, millions of them with millions, hundreds of millions, trillions of these rotten small crabs all over their little no-faces? You know that? And they were all weeping bitterly at their desks with their Fund heads in their Fund hands until they found their Fund mojo back and then went to me in this office and that office, in that corridor and that corridor and that floor and that floor of that multistory building, going: 'Say, Rinner, you heard the one about the crippled crab?' 'Yeah, yeah,' I said. But they all went raucous anyway going, 'It travelled from Melbourne to Sydney on a crutch'.

   (*Now he just nods when he hears the drum roll again. He rises and shuffles over to centre stage where SHEM has reappeared.*

   He drills out a few quick magic tricks… pulling coloured clothes out of RINNER's fly and out of his nose… pulling out polka dot boxer shorts out of his trousers etc before he

90

uses scissors to cut through the clown's braces, revealing the polka dot bloomers still on and scrawny legs...

An added bonus for SHEM is that he can make the greatest merriment from the fact that RINNER is standing them shamed, having peed himself.

At this public ridicule, CINNAMON moves out of the shadows, comes over slaps her brother across the face. This is not pretense.

There is an embarrassed silence.

She lays the back of her hand on RINNER's cheek pityingly... but still turns and goes back to WEYDOM where:

She could well be leading, but is definitely not resisting, going off with WEYDOM. There is no mistaking the intimacy of this.

RINNER dully watches them for an uncomprehending moment.

Then he tries to spring into life, tries to 'catch' their moving silhouettes. But he gets himself into such a state that he is literally running on the spot as frantically as his outfit allows.

SHEM forcibly brings him to a halt and then, equally as forcible, cranes Petey the Clown's head back to the audience. He has to do this three times before RINNER stays still awaiting what is to come.

All RINNER seems now to be able to do is laugh that selfsame bitter laugh that shocked CINNAMON, but SHEM is already producing another egg

This time he holds it above Petey-the-Clown's head will-I, won't-I? A drum roll gives him the answer.

91

As he smashes this egg down upon RINNER's head with an unprecedented intended violence, SHEM is loudly urging the rooster to crow by acting the hen as CINNAMON did earlier;)

SHEM: Bok, bok, bok... Clown, crow! Bok, bok...

It comes. It comes guttural at first, roughly cutting through the swollen silence and swells out of RINNER's mouth out of an awful pain. He is looking towards where CINNAMON has gone...)

RINNER: Cockle-doodle-doo!
  (*and finally*)
 COCKLE-DOODLE-DOO! COCKLE-DOODLE-DOO!

(He keeps mouthing this as the lighting gradually fades from him.

Blackout)

22.

(Without the collar and nose and shoes of Petey the Clown but still in the clown's clothes, RINNER sits against the wall beneath the mirror.

There is a long and isolating pause.

He occasionally nods to himself as if realising he is now alone.

Finally, it seems he is duty bound to stand and confront the mirror for a stand-up routine. While it mimics a stand-up comedian, it is delivered monotonously, without humour)

RINNER: Hellohellohello. You take my Mum… any takers?...
no?... what need more heavy lifting steroids? So she gave up
buying lottery tickets after she had me. Took up Russian roulette
instead. She said my Dad left town on the next train before what
she had to have me she didn't pass on to him. He took all the
money she had in her cookie jar for *her* train out. After she kissed
me for the first time she didn't kiss me again until I was eighteen.
Said in between was the longest spit she'd ever had. Not that I
had a deprived upbringing. My Mum wrote to me every day.
She'd slip an IOU made out to her from me under my bedroom
door every night when she was going to bed. She'd sign off, The
Dropsy Tragic. When I started to bring girls home, she made them
go through a sheep dip. After they'd gone, they'd find one of her
disclaimer forms in their handbags. At the age of eight, she
brought me a pet. It was a king cobra. She said if I was a good
boy she'd buy it a cage rather than under my bed. She'd send me
off the school with a 'To Let' sign around my neck. From the day
she had me, her brother tried to spirit her out of the Maternity
ward, but they were stopped and told by the staff it was all out or
none out. She only came back in when they promised her a daily
bath in holy water. They kept that promise too until they found
the hospital chaplain in there with her one day. When she went to
work, she was so keen to leave me she'd take her cut lunch in a
packed suitcase. When she registered my name with Kids
Welfare, she filed a defamation suit at the same time. She settled
when they promised that Australia would never remember a thing
about me and the Maternity joint needn't be burnt down. Did I tell
you the one about the guy talking to a mirror, going, 'Mirror,
mirror, I'm in…

(Stops. Has a coughing fit, which lays him low to sit up
against the wall under the mirror again.

This time there are unmistakable sounds of an airport.

He does not move, not even his head much, when the others,
as a tour group, file past on their journeys one by one.

First there is MURIEL strolling by. As the others will come
to do, she breaks away from a shadowy gaggle. She kneels

93

by him, takes off her wig and puts it in his lap:)

MURIEL: Rinny my lovely couldn't-take-the-pace, I keep telling all my males: there's no need to sink until you can't stop shrinking. But I'll be waiting; I won't let you down.

RINNER: Judge, did I ever belong outside?

MURIEL: (shaking head) There are too many of those children out there, my cluckie.

RINNER: Did I ever belong inside?

MURIEL: (shrugging) There are probably too many of those children inside too, my cluckie.

RINNER: Can't you even say I once did?

MURIEL: What can I say on the court record, my Rinny-pull-through?

RINNER: Didn't I love enough?

MURIEL: I wouldn't have thought so.

RINNER: Then where do I belong?

MURIEL: How's about just where you are?
   (*he nods*)
Oh, and I've been told to tell you:
Our Petey the Clown's gone done all the rounds
When they found him in pieces
He expounded the thesis
He was even more fragmented than ever before.

THE SHADOWS GAGGLE*: (chorus)*
Oh, the head on his shoulders
Made such a lot of pearler boulders.

94

MURIEL: And here's your Mr When-he-plays-with-himself-you-lose-the-point Black Blank-eyes himself…

(As she returns to the shadow gaggles, pointing out WEYDOM as he next breaks away to take her place)

WEYDOM: You're a hard man to follow, old son, but that's because you might really think you're leaning up against a sea wall or something, but it's really the airport. Your solar system's just on the fritz, cocko. You're really getting on that plane even though I've shopped you to the Indonesians, aren't you? Of course you are. Remember when you're in death row: all martyr pots aren't to pee in, you know. Here's the lady of love…

(CINNAMON takes his place)

CINNAMON: Oh, I didn't realise. Professor, I am so sorry for getting your expectations up.
  (song lilt)
I can't help it.

RINNER: Marlene Dietrich wrote that.

CINNAMON: Oh, and *I* was told to tell you:
oh, twill triluna trystful while the trust whimsies true…

RINNER: I wrote that.

CINNAMON: But I was better at using it, don't you think?

(A summoning drum roll)

CINNAMON: I must go.

 RINNER: That's okay. Cinnamon of the fireflighty nights.

CINNAMON: Sir Ex-ness. Professor.

(She leans down and kisses the top of his head.

SHEM takes her place)

SHEM: Yeh, cocklehead! You should get into show time, bub. Come'n'see us sometimes when you've got no time to spend on anything else but your crowing.
(*he magic-tricks a clown's red button nose out of RINNER's ear*)
Hey, the last one wore this thought he was king of the chook house but he was just a sheikh to his bones.
(*squeezing rubber nose*)
Honk, honk. Man with missing parts coming on through.

RINNER: Shem it's a shame.

SHEM: Too right, cocklehead. You leave the real Abos stuff to us full bloods and you'll be jackie.

(He places a child's Land-Rights flag in RINNER's hand)

SHEM: Try not to dribble on that, okay?

(MAIYAH and HUKKA next come together from out of the gaggle)

MAIYAH: No get jealous. But he never stop telephone call. I say no Dee Rinner al' time; he go cough, cough, wheeze al' time moonlight dinner. I say him, hey who pay for damage inner spring mattress?

HUKKA You hear someone say quick go for the hole in the wire, you go for it, bub. That's what I told him.

MAIYAH: Give him five dollar.

HUKKA: You give him five dollars.

MAIYAH: Give him five dollar he give me.

HUKKA: Here, bub, take a fiver; go spend it on some Serious Matter and trouble us no more.

MAIYAH: Velly elegrant.

(HUKKA pulls the dollar note back from RINNER. He has had it on a string)

MAIYAH: Boy, wha' a loser.

(The two leave together. When they return to the gaggle, ALI breaks off and moves towards him, but stops nearby – half in and half out of the shadows -- without going too near him.

RINNER doesn't have to look up to know she is there. At first he can only nod away)

RINNER: (finally able to muster:) Darling Ali, don't forget the compassionate. The sweetest of things that you are. The trouble was always the dying around me, and I'm sorry. But the thing to do is to replace it all with a bit of the old oxygen, don't you think? Does wonders for the heart. You are my Ali.

(ALI taps him on the shoulder so that he finally looks up into her eyes. He has tears in his. She makes fangs with her fingers and taps her throat and shrugs 'sorry, I can't speak', then she re-emerges into the gather gaggle of shadows.

In her place, and piteously so, comes DEE)

DEE: What are you doing down here, Dar?

RINNER: Scratching my navel. I'm going to lose you again, aren't I?

DEE: To be perfectly honest, I don't know. Out on a bit of a wander a bit too far. But it's so lovely up here knowing my old Dar is where I can find him.

RINNER: I broke my ankle.

97

DEE: No, you didn't, silly.

RINNER: I did. I told you it was attached to my body by pain from the ankle up.

> *(She kneels down to touch his outstretched feed in the manner of Indian respect. Then turns and returns to the shadows.*
>
> *Her advent gives him some sort of energy. He goes to speak, cannot manage it just then. Yet, as the lighting fades to a mere spot on him, he manages to crawl over to the phone in the middle of his apartment floor. Once there, much is restored, however temporarily...)*

RINNER: What I was saying, little my girlie, is there's this apartment door your silly old Dad has locked his keys in and there's that outer door there where he's locked his keys in and then that outer door to the street he's locked his keys in and the bomb of a car he's locked the keys in that hasn't got a lock left anyway, not to mention the garage and the key I forgot I locked in in there. You might be thinking that can't be right; you can't lock your keys *in* surely. Well, I can. Your old Dad can, and you're thinking there can't be absolutely nobody around who can't help with a key here or there, but you'd be mightily mistaken. You don't know what tricks mirrors can play.
> *(then)*
The real reason I wanted to talk to you now before next week is when, in all the swim, it came to keys and all God's little children and Boris the pigs...you see, don't you?... *I was never intelligent enough!*
> *(quietens himself)*
It's just that I think I'm really hurting now. I think something from the ankle up's slipped its bonds, you know? But I just rang to tell you while the going was good that when they took Caesar's knife to our Ali hoping they weren't too late for you from the poison... you see... what a father I would have made if only you had survived.

(Lighting fades on him, staring ahead)

RINNER: So the guy says to the mirror, 'Mirror, mirror, I've gone and fallen in love. Am I crazy?' and the mirror says, 'Of course not; love is a wonder', but before the guy can leave it adds, 'What's crazy is not so much asking a mirror, but having to wear a red rubber nose to look yourself in the eye'.

(long fixed-stare pause.

He moves away from the mirror, and defeatedly shuffles back to the wheelchair at the back, where he sits in pale light that is, anyway, fading from him.

He nods at the last when CINNAMON's Billie Holliday's song comes up:
I'll be seeing you
In all the old familiar places
That this heart of mine embraces
All day and through.

In that small café
The park across the way
The children's carousel
The chestnut trees. The wishing well...)

(End)

About the author

Bill Reed is a novelist, playwright and short-story writer. He was born in Perth, Australia, but grew up in Adelaide and Melbourne, where he is better known as a local author. His nine professionally-produced plays include *Burke's Company*, *Mr Siggie Morrison with his Comb and Paper*, *Truganinni*, *Cass Butcher Bunting*. These plays have also been published. His twelve novels have included *Dogod*, *Lankan 1001 Nights Part 1 and Part 2, White Wi, Me the Old Man*, and the novel loosely-based tetralogy *Throw Her Back, Are Your Human?, Awash and Tasker Tusker Tasker*.

The Australian Script Centre has accepted 23 of his plays for listing and purchase through its official website Australianplays.org.

He has worked as editor and journalist both in Australia and overseas. In Australia, he has been Publishing Manager of such major book-publishing houses as Rigby, A.H. and A.W. Reed, and the Macmillan Company of Australia. His novel *Stigmata* won the Fellowship of Australian Writers' ANA award. Among his awards for drama are Critics Choice and The Alexander Theatre Award for *Burke's Company* and *Cass Butcher Bunting* respectively. He has won national competitions in all three categories of drama, novels and short stories, including the National Short Story Award.

He now divides his time between his native Australia and Sri Lanka.

Critics on Bill Reed

'Bill Reed is a major Australian author... one might find much of his writing Joycean, some of it Kafkaish and mostly all Rabelaisean. Yet it remains uniquely his own very Australian voice... a great writer... a great original'
  Nadine Amadio, Arts National

On STIGMATA
'Stigmata is a compelling Australian novel with the kind of piercing emotional power that illuminated Patrick White's writing.'
  Review, Sunday Telegraph
'Challenges comparison with Faulkner, not to mention Patrick White.'
  Veronica Brady, Australian Book Review
'Bill Reed's characters bear stigmata, like Patrick White's "the burnt ones", but there is nothing derivative about Reed's highly original and forceful style, nor his driven, anguished characters.'
  Helen Daniel, the Age

On ME, THE OLD MAN
'Like certain Samuel Beckett novels, it could have left the reader feeling suicidal but in fact the final effect is one of driving elation.'
  Jill Neville, Sydney Morning Herald

On IHE
'IHE is a fabulous comic creation.'
  Helen Daniel, The Age

On CROOKS
'... totally uninhibited, Rabelasian and inventive'
  Elizabeth Riddell, Bulletin Magazine
'Reed has a great comic gift. Crooks is a very funny book. An hilarious and outrageous book.'
  Nadine Amadio, Arts National

On TUSK
'A fascinating hybrid of political thriller and metaphysical fable.'

Andrew Riemer, Sydney Morning Herald

'Tusk is one of those rare novels that really deserves an immediate re-reading. It is complex, multi-layered, and a superb psychological puzzle.'

Rosser Street, The Australian